Hey, I'd Eat This at Home!

A Fresh and Fearless Approach to Wilderness and Home Cooking

MICHAEL GRAY

UNCOMMON PRESS
Beulah, Michigan

UNCOMMON PRESS
www.uncommonadv.com

First Edition, First Printing

Gray, Michael L., 1960-

　　Hey, I'd eat this at home! : a fresh and fearless approach to wilderness and home cooking / Michael Gray. — 1st ed. — Beulah, Mich. : Uncommon Press, c2010.

　　　　p. ; cm.
　　　　ISBN: 978-0-9828196-0-9
　　　　Includes bibliographical references and index.

　　　　1. Outdoor cooking. 2. Quick and easy cooking. 3. Camping—Equipment and supplies. 4. Cookbooks. I. Title.

TX823 .G73 2010　　　　2010930768
641.5/78—dc22　　　　1009

Cover painting: Ofra Svorai of www.ofrastudio.com

Illustrations: Steve Gilzow

Photos: Dietrich Floeter of www.dietrichfloeter.com

Text design: Mary Jo Zazueta of www.tothepointsolutions.com

Printed in the United States of America.

10 9 8 7 6 5 4 3 2 1

FSC
Mixed Sources
Product group from well-managed
forests and other controlled sources

Cert no. SW-COC-002283
www.fsc.org
© 1996 Forest Stewardship Council

This book is dedicated to everyone with whom I have had the pleasure and privilege of sharing wild places.

Dinner . . . Lake Superior style.

Caveats, Disclaimers, and General Attempts to Dodge Responsibility

THIS BOOK TAKES a think-for-yourself approach to food and camping craft. Popular opinion about nutrition changes as frequently as innovations in equipment for outdoor adventures. Because of these rapid changes and the accelerated rate people can acquire information via the Internet, I take a general approach to equipment and meal selection.

I do not discuss nutritional values or caloric intake recommendations for different sports, gear guides, etc. In other words, I won't bog you down with fad diets and nano-gear widgetry.

All that said, it is time to launch into the book . . .

CONTENTS

PART ONE: BE PREPARED

PART TWO: LET'S COOK

FOREWORD

by Nigel Foster

FOR MOST PEOPLE, being comfortable at home is easy. Fancy a snack? Stroll to the kitchen; take a knife from the drawer to slice what's left of the loaf of bread. You'd like something with it? Grab some cheese and salad from the fridge, and whatever else looks good. It doesn't take much. When the ingredients are gone, you can run to the store for more. Away from home those familiar routines change. You paddled or hiked to this pristine beach, nobody in sight, and you want a snack. You could eat anything, but your choices are limited to what you brought. Actually that's not entirely true. Your choices are limited by the ingredients you have, but the greater your imagination, the more choices you have.

I've known Michael Gray for more years than I have fingers, and I've run into him in all corners of the country in different seasons. He is like a monarch butterfly, with north-south migration routes on both the east and west coasts. Wherever he pauses, he unpacks a little food, a zip-lock with something marinating inside, a tiny bottle of olive oil, a remnant of a smoked fish. Want to eat? Out comes a small cutting board, a sharp knife, a clove of garlic, and half a red pepper; next a small pan and a burner. Within a few minutes the smell of gourmet cooking rises into the air. We could be outside a cabin in South Carolina or on an Oregon beach—it doesn't matter. It is the same kind of experience. Michael knows how to combine whatever simple ingredients he has into enticing dishes, wherever he is, and he knows how to carry all he needs.

Michael's expeditions, camp-cooking demonstrations, and seminars at sea-kayaking symposia have become legendary. They are so popular that people often don't realize Michael belongs on the outside of the seminar tent, not inside. What he shares in techniques and tips, what he rustles up with a pinch of seasoning, is what he rustles up when he is in his real element: multi-day sea kayaking or canoeing, hiking, fly-fishing or simply on the road. He eats well wherever he is.

Being realistic, he needs to know how much he must carry if he is only catering for himself or how that changes if he is with five others. He needs to know when to eat things, which ingredients will still be edible after a week on the water, and which herbs and spices are easy to carry. Cooking on expedition is an art. You carry everything so you do not want to waste anything. Leftovers are like the dollars in change from a twenty dollar bill. Michael is the ultimate make-a-meal-out-of-leftovers cook.

For years people have asked Michael how they might remember all the tips and tricks, the details they need to know to cook like he does. "I'll write a book!" he'd reply with a laugh! For years people asked "Have you finished that book yet?" He'd grimace. Writing a book is like raising a child, with all the awkwardness and joy and investment of time. It took years before Michael finally settled down to it. Now he has achieved a monumental task, grabbing a many-legged monster and pressing it between covers.

The essence of Michael's wilderness catering, food preparation, cooking, and seasoning is here, along with a series of recipe ideas. Browse the book, pick a recipe you fancy, and jump into it with both feet! The world of living out and living it up is all yours!

ACKNOWLEDGMENTS

ALTHOUGH THIS WRITING venture has been fueled and inspired by guests on my trips over nearly thirty years, it wouldn't have come together without the efforts of my paddling family. This project has been borne out of efforts of paddlers for the most part.

Thanks to Nigel Foster, dear friend and gifted finder of mushrooms, for the well-placed boot that started this ball rolling toward completion.

To Russell Farrow, paddling Rock Star, for the backward . . . we are paddlers after all.

To Ofra Svorai, whose watercolors of Georgian Bay are inspired by her canoe trips there. Find her unique watercolors at ofrastudio.com.

To Steve Gilzow, for his beautifully rendered icons and drawings of the Kingfisher that flits through these pages.

To Dietrich Floeter, for all of the photographs used inside this book.

To my friends Fred and Kathy for the photo of me on the back-cover.

To Kathleen Hibbard, Nancy Thornton, Sharon Bustamante and a number of others who have shared their inspiration and recipes.

Thanks to the Skrocki clan for Sunday dinners, an infinite number of warm hugs and positive encouragement.

To my dear friend and quasi-sister, Juliet, thanks for her sharp mind, educated palate, and support to finish this book.

This book would not have happened without the energies of

Mary Jo Zazueta for hand-walking me through the book-making process. Thanks for her patience and efforts to bring my words in from the wild.

Thanks to my proofreaders—Claud Agnello, Sharon Bustamante, and Barb Osborn—and proof-eaters to get this into understandable form.

Lastly, but mostly, thanks to all of those who had faith that this project would ever come to fruition and actually paid for it in advance . . . now, that's pressure.

INTRODUCTION

SOME PEOPLE LOOK at mountains and as their gaze travels upward they think about climbing the peaks. My eyes are drawn to the valleys where those mountains meet their siblings—because I know there is water there. Water that eventually finds its way to a sea.

Whether paddling or hiking, water is the magnet that has guided me along a life of adventure and great lessons. This watery path has taken me all over the world, and in my travels I have always enjoyed the company of a flashy, raucous companion bird that makes its living on water, too. That is why you will find a Kingfisher motif guiding you through the pages of this book. The chatter of that bird, as it capers through the air, always reminds me to be in the present. There is a common thread among the outdoor people I've known: they have learned to focus in the present enough to see where they are ... they savor it all, the view and the meal. Nothing screams "BE HERE!" as much as something amazing hitting your palate.

ANATOMY OF A RECIPE PAGE

Backpack

Base Camp

Canoe

Kayak

Vegetarian
V = Vegan

EACH RECIPE IS indexed by icon (see above) to indicate what activities it is best-suited for and whether it is vegetarian and/or vegan friendly. Under the recipe title you will find preparation time, type of cookware needed, and directions on what to do at home and in camp to turn this into an appealing meal.

Each recipe includes a shopping list of the ingredients required to serve two, four, six, and twelve people plus suggestions on how to lighten weights and adjust a recipe to your personal tastes. The recipes contain the following information:

- **Icons:** specify what activities the recipe is best suited for.

- **Prep Time:** estimated time to aid you with meal planning.

- **At Home:** the tasks you should take care of prior to your trip.

- **In Camp:** simple instructions on how to prepare each recipe in the field.

- **Shopping List:** a table that shows how much of each ingredient is needed to feed different sized groups.

- **Variations and Comments:** ideas for adapting the recipe to meet different tastes and needs.

HOW TO USE THIS GUIDE

OUR LIVES ARE FULL of things beyond our control, and those factors have an even greater impact when we are in the backcountry. We can't control the weather, critters, or personalities—but over the years I have learned that the aroma of Georgia Peach Cake baking in the wilderness can make people forget about challenging weather and bugs.

Good food is also a safety device. You don't believe me? With certain groups, if I forget the chocolate my life may be in grave danger. Thus, I think of tasty food as trip insurance.

In my early days of outfitting and guiding wilderness trips, the highest compliment to the menu was, "Hey, I'd eat this at home!" As time went on and my recipes developed, I heard "This is better than I eat at home!" Now my backcountry culinary skills have reached the point where the reactions are often, "Boy, when we get back, eating out is sure going to be a letdown!"

This is good. As a guide, I want my meals to elicit that kind of sentiment.

However, I have made a tragic error. You see, several thousand people throughout the country have eaten my cooking, either on expeditions or at outdoor-cooking demonstrations. And for years I told them, "Yes, I will put all of my recipes and cooking tips in a book." Well, many have grown tired of waiting; so it is now put-up or shut-up time—to save myself from being lynched.

Time has a way of morphing things beyond their original boundaries and such has been the case with this project. During its slow simmer, this book has grown to include food tips and tales from nearly thirty years of guiding and almost one hundred original recipes. My approach to this book—and life in general—isn't simple and fast, but rather substantial and celebratory.

Some recipes are lightweight and compact; others are more substantial and take advantage of fresh foods. The recipes rely on minimally processed ingredients that are commonly found in your local supermarket. They are meant to be flexible and fun. Go at them with gusto and they will serve you and those you feed well.

If you would like the convenience of a complete menu rather than searching through individual recipes, please refer to Appendix A on page 163. And, if you are primarily interested in this as a home cookbook, simply flip back to the recipes and be fearless.

Have fun and don't worry, this is recreation.

PART ONE

Be Prepared

Saved by Wonder Bread

Guides "on holiday" are often ill-prepared for emergencies . . .

One sunny afternoon, my friend Fred and I were enjoying a paddle on a Michigan river. We ate a "guy lunch" along the bank: bratwurst on a stick, fire, buns and beer. As we loaded up Roadkill, my old canoe, we noticed the shadows getting a little long and decided we'd better hustle to the take-out.

Roadkill *had been a forty-pound Kevlar beauty in her day, but she was a bit past her sell-by date. The areas between her patches were brittle as eggshells. Fred and I cruised along, waking turtles off their logs. Then we met with a reasonably stationary limb lurking just below the surface. From my seat in the back of the boat, I had a decent view of the geyser spurting up from the two-by-six-inch rift in the floor. Fred and I exchanged a few stressed words and managed to back off the limb and ease over to the riverbank before* Roadkill *was completely swamped.*

I didn't have my repair kit—no, not even duct tape. Hey, it was a day off. So, after emptying the canoe of all its contents, turning it over and drying it, we assessed our worldly goods to see if we could MacGyver our way out of a long walk through a swamp.

We settled on a lone hot dog bun. We stuck the bun in a zip-seal bag, inflated it with air, and stuffed it in the gash, hoping this would stem most of the flow. Then, we paddled like hell. If we shifted our weight away from the gash, we could make a good 300 meters before Fred had to bail the deep end. We managed to paddle the last fives miles rather quickly—with our honor intact and a story to share.

Saved by Wonder bread … only in Michigan.

Chapter 1

FUEL FOR THE JOURNEY: NUTRITION

ALTHOUGH OUR CULTURE SEEMS to be focused on low-carb diets—which is fine if you are driving a desk for a living—you are going to need on-demand energy for active outdoor pursuits. That's right, that brownie could be considered safety gear. Especially for the cook if the weather turns ugly.

Without sitting down to crunch the numbers, I think you will find that most of the recipes in this book have a good balance of carbohydrate-fat-protein ratios to help you make the most of your adventures. Most of the recipes and food plans start with a complex carbohydrate base with a balance of protein additives that come from vegetable protein complements, meat, dairy, and nuts. More than simply fuel to move your body, start thinking about great meals that move your spirit as well.

Carbohydrate Foundations
- **Pasta:** many shapes to play with, from orzo to couscous to tortellini
- **Rice:** white to basmati brown to wild to minute
- **Legumes:** all manner of beans, including lentils, peanuts, split peas, and garbanzos

- **Breads**: the more whole grain the better, includes bagels, lavash, pita, biscuits, crackers, tortillas
- **Grains**: bulgur, millet, barley, oats, corn, quinoa, buckwheat

Fruits and Vegetables (that don't require refrigeration)
- **Fresh Fruits**: apples, citrus, melons, pineapples, even bananas (just mash them into pancakes if they become abused)
- **Dried Fruits**: cherries, apples, blueberries, cranberries, prunes, raisins, apricots
- **Savory Veggies**: sweet and hot peppers, onions, garlic, squash
- **Staples**: potatoes, carrots, cabbages of all types, yams

Protein Additives
- **Meat & Fish**: vacuum-sealed smoked meats like salmon, turkey, and cured ham; various Italian cured sausages, like salami; freshly caught fish; canned or packet meats including fish, chicken, turkey, salmon, crabmeat, smoked oysters, and clams
- **Nuts**: add a nice crunchy texture to soft food
- **Dairy Products and Eggs**: various hard and cream cheeses travel well. Eggs travel well when left in their shells, do not require refrigeration, and are versatile. **Milk, either** canned, ultra-high temperature (UHT), or powdered whole milk.

Fats and Sugars
Also known as dessert; can keep you alive if someone is feeling chocolate-deprived.

- **Instant**: cheesecake mixes, peanut-butter pie, puddings, hard chocolate bars
- **Freshly baked**: brownies, cakes, cinnamon rolls, and cobblers
- **Hot drinks**: coffee, tea, chocolate, and cider are easy and quick mood-enhancers

Chapter 2

THE FIVE P'S:
PROPER PLANNING PREVENTS
POOR PERFORMANCE

Pantry Method

IN THE CASE OF TRIPS LONGER than one week, it is often practical to take more of a pantry approach, which involves packing a
variety of bulk items (usually dry) with no specific daily menu plan.
You more or less wing it as the day or activity permits. This does require
a bit of cooking skill, some imagination, and a good guide like the
NOLS (National Outdoor Leadership School) *Cookbook*. NOLS courses
are often 3 weeks or more in duration, which warrants this method.

Planned Menu/Pantry Combo

Since most of us do not take trips longer than a week in the backcountry, the approach in this guide is a hybridized version of pantry
method and individual meal planning that comes from thirty years of
in-field experience. It is really quite simple: the more work you do
ahead of time, the more time you will have to enjoy the place you're
in. Regardless of the destination, the better laid your groundwork, the
greater likelihood of a fulfilling experience. This does not mean you
should have everything planned down to the last minute or set high

expectations about small details—ultimately the world does not work that way. It simply means you should do as much of the work ahead of time as possible and be flexible with your meals. Select a good destination, choose well your fellow travelers, pick a pace that works for all, have an optimum time frame lined up, and blend that with great food—then you will have the trip of a lifetime.

Start with menu planning. Research your fellow travelers' food restrictions and passions and build a flexible menu that matches the pace and effort expenditures on the trip. This also helps you retain the magic of spontaneity on a trip.

Packaging Provisions for Portability

A great deal of refuse is generated by disposable packaging materials. This may be a small issue at home but it is a much larger item to sidestep for backcountry travel. Why take trash into the backcountry in the first place? When prepping for a backcountry trip, reduce packaging before you travel. For example, if you have a prepared mix, like brownies, remove the outer box, put the inner bag into a heavy-duty zip-seal plastic bag, add the cutout directions, and label the outside of the bag with a Sharpie marker. The labeling could be critical later when trying to discern pancake mix from hummus.

Added bonus: a zip-seal plastic bag makes a convenient mixing container for batter.

Bulk Foods

It is often possible to purchase bulk dry goods at food cooperatives and large grocery chains. You can find items like rice, grains, pancake and biscuit mix, spices, dehydrated cooked bean mixes, cereals, nuts, hummus, and dried vegetables available in bins. In addition to lightening your "de-packaging" workload, it gives you the opportunity to purchase only what you need for each recipe.

Breakfast and Lunch

Breakfasts and lunches are birthed from a pair of grab bags of raw materials. Pancake mix, cereals, nuts, bagels, pita bread, crackers, cheese, nut butters, and hot drinks are packaged as either breakfast or lunch in loose, malleable stuff sacks. This makes them easy to pack and transport to your kitchen.

Remember last in first out (LIFO) when packing items; so coffee will be the first thing your caffeine-deprived brain encounters when peeking into the breakfast bag.

Dinners

Package dinners by meal and sequence in such a way that leftovers are easily cycled into the next meal. Example: one evening's leftover black beans become *huevos rancheros* the next morning. Another important item to be mindful of is to plan meals that take less preparation time for days when you are likely to have less energy and time. When packing for a trip, lay out a series of breathable bags marked dinner #1, #2, and so on for the number of days you are going to be out. Ingredients for each of these meals, including dessert, will be packed in the bag with the exception of your spices (separate kit), and any perishables that you may have in your "cheater pack" (see below). When it is time to prepare the first dinner, you grab dinner #1 and your spice kit and that ends your search. No more hungry, frustrated searches rummaging through packs and kayak hatches. Meals come together more quickly and with a much higher fun factor.

Coolers or the "Cheater Pack"

For some of the most perishable items—cheat. On sea-kayak trips and river trips where weight isn't a big concern, carry a "cheater pack"—a soft-sided, durable 15- to 20-quart cooler containing several frozen items with the most sensitive produce on top. Romaine lettuce, snow peas, berries, and fresh herbs live significantly longer due to such blatant exploitation of "the rules." Frozen block ice lasts the longest; I simply freeze potable water in plastic two-quart milk jugs for an ice supply. The melt water doesn't spoil the food and I can use it later. Freezing canned beer (really) or using frozen meats, juices, and berries make nice treats later and create more cold-thermal mass. I have even used dry ice to keep ice cream frozen for a surprise fortieth birthday strawberry sundae on day three of a paddling trip in the Florida Keys.

The Spice Kit: Food First Aid

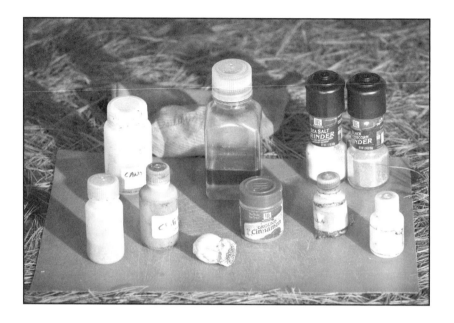

Liquids

Liquids have a nasty habit of escaping; so a collection of wide-mouth Nalgene® bottles in various sizes does an excellent job of containment. I pack the bottles in a zip-seal bag for extra insurance. And, if you label the bottle with a Sharpie, be sure to cover your writing with a strip of clear packing tape to prevent the oils from smearing your labeling efforts. Here are some handy choices:

- ❐ Canola or peanut oil
- ❐ Honey or Maple syrup
- ❐ Olive oil
- ❐ Soy or Tamari sauce
- ❐ Vanilla extract (go for the real thing)
- ❐ Worcestershire sauce

The Five P's: Proper Planning Prevents Poor Performance

Spices

Dry spices can easily be stored in refillable plastic containers. Be sure to label them well and cover the labels with a protective film of clear tape so you can decipher them over time.

- [ ] Basil
- [ ] Black Pepper in a small refillable grinder
- [ ] Cinnamon
- [ ] Chili Powder
- [ ] Cumin
- [ ] Nutmeg
- [ ] Oregano
- [ ] Salt

If you have the room, you may want to add other spices like Cajun, thyme, or rosemary. Dry onion flakes and dry garlic also have their place, but there is nothing like using the real thing for the best flavor—and fresh garlic is very portable.

Chapter 3

THE BACKCOUNTRY KITCHEN

TO PREPARE TERRIFIC backcountry meals in a variety of settings, there are some basic tools and equipment you will need. I will start with the base-camp kitchen and work toward more minimalist kitchens designed for lighter-weight wilderness travel.

"Base camp" might sound like you are preparing to make an attempt to climb Mt. Everest—but have you ever tried to feed a group of ten in the backcountry? In this book, base camp is tailored for car camping and other excursions where space and weight are not as limited. (Please refer to Appendix A for sources on where to find the outdoor cooking equipment mentioned in this book.)

The Base-Camp Kitchen

This kitchen setup works well when I guide coastal-kayak and canoe tours for groups of up to twelve. Everything nests together, which keeps it manageable no matter how I transport the equipment. And, even though it is a pretty big unit, I am able to store it in the front hatch of my sea kayak. Start by using a small- to medium-sized nylon mesh bag—the type you can find at a river supply company.

- ❒ Insert a stack of plastic dinner plates, one per crew member, and include an extra one to use for food preparation.
- ❒ Next insert a ten-inch frying pan without a handle (Banks Fry-Bake Pan).

- ❏ Onto that stack a pot set (mine consists of the following):
  - ❏ A large steamer pot (8- to 12-quart) that can be used to boil pasta, keep food warm, steam tortillas, bake, etc.
  - ❏ Nested in this are two small stainless steel pots with lids that are used to heat water, cook cereals and sauces, and act as mixing bowls.
  - ❏ Nested inside the inner pots is a set of bowls.
  - ❏ Wrapped around the bowls is a flexible plastic cutting board.
  - ❏ There will be a few nooks and crannies in this puzzle into which you can tuck a couple kitchen towels and a dish cleaning kit comprised of small container of biodegradable soap, a small plastic bottle of bleach and a pot scrubber. Add a silicone kitchen mitt to use as a hot pad for a professional touch. Toss in your utensil kit and water filter system and you've got a portable kitchen that will get the job done for a large crew.

The Small-Group Kitchen

This equipment handles up to six campers and the smaller package can easily be stored in packs or kayak hatches. Again, start with a handy nylon mesh bag.

- ❏ Insert an appropriate number of plates for your crew plus one extra.
- ❏ Next, add the same 10-inch frying pan.
- ❏ Nested into that is a pair of nesting pots, approximately 8-quarts in size.
- ❏ Flexible plastic cutting board.

❒ A few lightweight plastic bowls that nest into each other and the two pots

❒ Dish-cleaning supplies

❒ Utensil Kit

❒ Water Filter System

The Backpacking Kitchen

This setup is ideal for one to four people; is lightweight and non-bulky. In a mesh bag insert:

❒ A lightweight 4-quart stainless steel pot with a lid

❒ For frying/toasting/warming a small frying pan with a lid (the smaller Banks Fry-Bake pan), or a small one with removable or folding handle

❒ High-sided Lexan plates/bowls

❒ Dish-cleaning supplies

❒ Utensil Kit

❒ Water Filter System

Utensil Kit

Depending on the size of the group and your destination, your utensil kit may be small and simple or grow exponentially for a base-camp setup. You can be as elaborate as you want. I have seen hand-cranked blenders, ice-cream makers, espresso makers, and coffee grinders for backcountry use. In any case, it is less work to use items that serve more than one purpose, i.e., you can MacGyver your way through a meal with a Swiss army knife or carry all the toys.

When cooking for a group of six or more, I carry a roll-up wrench bag from a tool company that contains:

❒ Metal pancake turner, cutter, scraper

❒ Large serving spoon, pot stirrer, scoop shovel

❒ Silicone spatula (Spoonula)

❒ Six-inch cook's knife

❒ Small ceramic draw-through knife sharpener

❒ Small metal whisk

❒ Pot grabs, multi-tool can opener

- A couple of extra spoons and forks (Lexan is light)
- Folded up aluminum windscreen
- Two butane lighters
- Hand Sanitizer
- Folding PVC bucket

For smaller groups and backpacking excursions, I pare this down to bare essentials. If I am using nonstick coated pans, I pack a lightweight plastic spoon and turner along with a less abrasive scrub pad.

POTS AND PANS

There is a wide variety of cookware available for backcountry use: stainless steel, aluminum, nonstick, hard-anodized, copper clad, titanium, unobtainium . . . you name it; if you want to spend the money, you can find it. You can buy complete sets, pots integrated with stoves, espresso makers, and even waffle irons! I've even seen a nice camping/outdoor cook set from Calphalon. It had me reaching for my credit card.

Based on my experience, here are some pros and cons of the different cooking materials:

- Aluminum with nonstick coating: lightweight with easy cleanup, but they scratch easily and don't brown food well
- Uncoated Aluminum: lightweight and distributes heat well but can be tough to clean and there is debate on the health risks of cooking with aluminum. (Unless camping is a fulltime life for you, get over it.) If you can pony up the funds, go for a product that is hard-anodized which provides a nonstick surface without the coatings to possibly dislodge into your diet.

- **Stainless steel**: durable, distributes heat pretty well, cleans up easily and doubles as a signaling device—but it is a bit on the heavy side
- **Titanium**: now you're just showing off

Pots

I favor pots with tight-fitting lids that can double as plates. Small diameter pots with taller profiles and flat bottoms balance better on one-burner stoves. New Zealanders call this style a "Billie." Billies are typically nested in sets and can sometimes be found in military surplus stores.

I often carry an 8-quart pasta boiler pot with a strainer insert. It may seem like a big piece of hardware but it makes straining noodles a lot safer, makes a great pancake and tortilla warmer (with a little hot water in the bottom), and everything else, including my Billie, fits inside it. I use a simple black-enameled-steel model.

Frying Pans

You can fry, brown, and toast using a pot, but what if it is busy doing other things? In that case you need a separate frying pan with a detachable or folding handle for ease of packing. The models with a folding handle and a nonstick coating might seem like a good idea, but they don't balance well on a one-burner stove, at least not with their handles sticking out waiting to catch a stray arm or an ankle. I prefer

There are two sizes of Fry-Bake pans available.

models with a hard-anodized surface that either have no handles or handles that can be removed. These are light, brown food well, and are fairly non-sticky.

Even though there is a wide range of outstanding products on the market, I still prefer my Banks Fry-Bake pan. It is light, versatile, easy-to-clean, perfectly sized, and has served me well for many years. (This terrific piece of gear is featured in greater detail in the baking chapter of this book.)

Complete Cookware Sets

In North America, both MSR and GSI offer a wide range of high-tech, integrated cookware that nest as complete sets, including plates and ergonomic mugs. They are space efficient, pricey, work well, look cool, and are a little silly. (Sometimes silly is a good thing.)

Sources for Outdoor Cookware

- Banks Fry-Bake Pans
  Frybake.com
- GSI Outdoors
  Gsioutdoors.com
- Jetboil
  Jetboil.com
- Mountain Safety
  Research (MSR)
  Cascadedesigns.com/msr
- Snow Peak
  Snowpeak.com
- The Woody
  uncommonadv.com

Cookware on the Cheap

Good quality castoffs from Mom can be useful with their handles removed. Secondhand shops in cities that are hubs for outdoor sports often yield some good finds; so the next time you are in Boulder, Durango, Santa Cruz, or even Traverse City, Michigan, visit the local Goodwill Store to see what outdoor treasures it may hold. Recycling isn't just for your rubbish. I scored some acrylic wine glasses last year!

THE MYSTICAL, THE SCARY, AND IMPOSSIBLE-TO-CARRY DUTCH OVEN

Usually starring center stage on float and horse-pack trips, the weighty Dutch oven is the source of some of the most deliriously tasty backcountry meals ever consumed. There are volumes of great books that raise this style of cooking to an art form. However, for backcountry excursions there are specially designed smaller and lighter ovens:

Woody's Outdoor Cookware Co.

Woody's oven was beautifully cast aluminum, 9-inches square, relatively light—and cooked like a dream. I have one; it will be in my will. By separating the two halves, you get a pair of frying pans, griddles, stir-frying pans, toasters, grills, and fajita pans that work well on one burner—or you can bake with it as a Dutch oven. From kayak ballast to bikini-waxing this thing has 1,001 uses; mine goes on every kayak trip with me. I even lugged it to New Zealand when I taught outdoor cookery at Nelson Polytech. There was a scramble for it when I departed. The bad news: they are no longer made. Even the foundry that cast it is past tense.

I'm getting ahead of myself—can't forget Woody himself. Woody Woodruff developed this oven for the Boy Scouts a half century ago. Although Woody and his oven are both gone, he leaves behind a lasting legacy in the form of his book, *Cooking the Dutch Oven Way*, which is a classic that has been updated and revised by his family. You can easily find the book on the Internet. It is worth collecting.

The New Woody

The good news: you can still get a Woody!

Glad I have your attention. Since you had the twisted sense to pick up this book and wade this far, you deserve some insider information. A few years ago, a creative and handsome devil named Rocky attended one of my cooking classes. After the class he asked if I was interested in producing this Dutch oven again. You bet I was. Together, Rocky and I redesigned the oven to work even better. It now fits in kayak hatches and is produced out of the same alloy as Dodge Viper engine blocks. True story. With this new design, it works easily on one-burner stoves. I use it during my outdoor cooking demonstrations and on all of my trips. Out of respect for Woody, Rocky and I named it after the dear man. He can take pride in knowing that his namesake will be making people happy in the backcountry for another half century.

Chapter 4

Camp Hygiene and Clean Water

Wash Your Hands

YOUR MOTHER WAS RIGHT. The easiest way to share unwanted bacteria with your friends is through the kitchen. To prevent this from occurring, keep your fingernails trimmed short and do a thorough scrub with antibacterial soap a good fifty paces from any fresh water source. Hand sanitizer gels can supplement the process and be a good touch-up between thorough washings. Try to find a gel that is unscented so it doesn't impart a foul flavor on your food or attract unwanted curious critters.

Note: Alcohol is the active ingredient in hand sanitizers, so expect your hands to get very dry unless you counteract the effects with moisturizers at the end of the day.

Cleaning Dishes

The dishwashing system I have used on our trips for the last twenty years is effective, simple, and easy. First, be sure the kitchen is located fifty paces or more from fresh water and at least that distance from the tents. "Why?" you ask. Stay tuned . . .

I start heating water while we eat. Once we are finished eating, the dirty dishes go through a three-step process:

① cold water pre-wash

② warm soapy wash

③ disinfectant rinse

A quick pre-wash is done over a large cooking pot (could be a used one). Be sure to contain all remaining food particles in the pot. Next, pour hot water into a large bowl with a soapy scrubbie and use that to do a thorough washing. Finally, the remaining warmed water is poured into a folding bucket with cold water and a little squirt of bleach for the rinse. If you wash a drinking cup first, you can use it to pour the disinfectant rinse over the soapy dishes at the rinse bucket. Deposit the clean dishes upside down in an empty mesh bag; when the bag is full, hang it on a tree branch to air dry. Giardia and most other nasty germs die off when they are dry.

Clean the cooking pots last and be sure to strain the food particles out of the pre-rinse to pack out with your trash. Broadcast the dishwater over a wide area well away from the tents. I've used this cleaning method with untreated water for years with good success. It is easy and as close to being fun as doing the dishes gets.

Drinking Water

You need clean drinking water to live. It is that simple. No matter how crystal clear and inviting a water source looks, you will never be sorry by erring on the side of caution. Ingesting the wrong lovely clear cup of water can slowly kill you—or make you wish for a swift end.

In backcountry situations you have several options for safe drinking water:

Boil: Bringing water to the boiling point will render it safe for drinking just about anywhere on this planet. That means the water you cook with is safe and doesn't need further treatment. The downsides to this method are that it is labor intensive, uses a lot of fuel, and produces flat-tasting drinking water.

Chemical treatment: Cheap, easy, and effective if you follow the directions. The downside is that it might not kill Cryptosporidium and it produces yucky-tasting water.

Mechanical filtration: Most backcountry travelers carry a water filter and there are many good units on the market. They filter out most of the nasty beasties that can do you harm and produce good-tasting water. The downside is that most of the mechanical filters do nothing for viruses and if used poorly they can actually increase your risk of getting sick. Fortunately, most North American backcountry water sources are free of viruses. Be sure to know how to repair your filter in the field and carry parts or a backup filter with you. One bad O-ring can ruin your trip. Ask NASA.

Proper Use of Water Filters

Think about it. All water filters have an intake hose that draws in potentially unsafe water and an outflow hose that deposits filtered water into your clean container. Over time, the intake hose takes in a large volume of water which can create concentrations of the gunk you are trying to filter out. Also, if the intake hose is stored with the rest of the unit, it can drool bits of nasty beasties all over the outflow parts. So, the moral of the story is to always flush your outflow system well with filtered water and follow the manufacturer's directions to periodically back flush and clean the filter.

Water Bottles and Hydration Bags

Share your experience but not your water bottle, lip balm, or partially eaten foodstuffs. This will aid in keeping unwanted hitchhikers to a minimum. The last few years have produced a plethora of hydration packs that utilize a bladder system with a hose terminated with a valve that you bite on to get a drink. They are a terrific way to keep gradually hydrated. But, what is going on inside that bladder while it waits for the next outing? Oh, and that hose dragging along behind the paddler in the Chicago River, the one with the bite valve porpoising playfully along? Could be a prelude to a date with a long-term antibiotic—or worse.

It is vitally important to follow the manufacturer's directions on cleaning and storing bladder hydration systems to keep them filling you with clean water rather than E. coli.

Camp Hygiene and Clean Water

The Straight Poop

There are manuals with sequels on how to shit in the woods. Plan ahead for your environment and leave as little poop in the wilderness as possible. Many coastal water trails and river management areas require visitors to pack out human waste; there are a number of manufactured and do-it-yourself (DIY) systems available for doing this.

In other areas, you can leave a lighter footprint on the environment by using the cat hole method: deposit your post-meal leavings in the top organic layers of the soil, cover well, and pack out your used paper in a brown paper sack (burnable) inside a zip-seal plastic bag, along with a tube of hand sanitizer. You should get at least one hundred feet away from any fresh water sources when you do this. Choose your spot well. One with a supportive branch, log, or a rock and a vista can provide a comfortable poo with a view.

Chapter 5

Now We're Cooking

A WORD ABOUT CAMPFIRE cooking: there is nothing like the romance of cooking over an open fire in the wilderness. The blackened pots, the burned fingers, the fire scars left in no longer unspoiled campsites . . . Yep, them were the days . . . the long-gone days of high impact and perceived unlimited resources.

The use of fire pans and ash removal cans required on river trips is a good example of low-impact fire use. There are even small portable folding fire pans and some patterns for do-it-yourselfers. Consult National Outdoor Leadership School (NOLS) texts for tips as they are the leader in leave-no-trace outdoor travel.

Stoves

There are a wide variety of convenient and easy-to-use lightweight stoves to aid us in leaving a lighter footprint on the environment. Stoves that have two speeds—off and blowtorch—are great for quickly boiling water, making instant soups, and welding. Most of the recipes in this book, however, require a stove that can do more. For your ascension to camp-chef status, you will need a stove that ranges from gentle simmer to raging Cajun. Weight, durability, size, and type of fuel are other attributes to consider. Make sure the stove is one you can repair in the field or bring a backup stove. Consider the fuel type that will work best for your trip and work backward from there to choose a model that satisfies your needs.

There are various stoves and fuels to choose from that pack up for easy transport. *Left to right:* Double-burner with propane tank, liquid fuel (Coleman), and iso-butane stove.

Fuel Types

- **Propane:** commonly available and convenient canister fuel for base camp/car camping stoves, but way too heavy for backcountry use.

- **Butane and its hybrids:** canister-style fuel found around the world in more populated areas. Stoves that use this are lightweight, adjustable, and compact. You can fly with these stoves since they separate from their fuel tanks and you can usually buy fuel at your destination—for a price. Downside? The fuel is expensive and you have to pack out the empty canisters.

- **White gas/Coleman fuel/naphtha:** common liquid fuel found throughout North America that is dispensed into purpose-built bottles that you carry. There are many stove choices for this type of fuel and it is relatively cheap, efficient, and reliable.  The downsides are that the stoves can be fussy, it spills, is hard to find internationally, and powers a number of those *off or blowtorch* models.

- **Auto gas/diesel/kerosene:** multi-fuel stoves that burn these types of fuel are popular with people who do a lot of international travel. The downsides are they burn very dirty, require a fair bit of cleaning, and sound like a jet taking off. The plus is they will burn almost anything with proper stove maintenance.

- **Alcohol:** this liquid is found the world over and fuels the simplest of stoves. Basically it is a tin of ethyl alcohol with a swinging flap over the top to control the flame. Beautiful in their simplicity, these stoves burn very clean and silently. There are cool models on the market, plus innumerable DIY possibilities. They don't burn very hot, evenly, or cook efficiently, but you have to love the low-tech simplicity.

Getting the Most From Your Stove

Use the cleanest fuel you can find and keep the jets and generator free of carbon buildup. In other words, follow the cleaning directions. And, keep the fuel tank properly pressurized on liquid fuel models. To get the most out of any stove, regardless of the type of fuel it requires, be sure to use a windscreen to keep the heat contained under the pots and pans. Wind robs stoves of efficiency more than any other single factor. If you don't use

a windscreen you could find yourself short of fuel. When setting up your stove, take care to balance it in a level and stable configuration to avoid accidents with boiling pots.

Kitchen Placement

Remember to position your kitchen well away from the tents and freshwater sources. Cooking and cleaning at least fifty paces from fresh water helps lessen your impact as well as protect the integrity of your water sources. Also, try to setup your kitchen on "durable surfaces" so that meal traffic doesn't leave heavy footprints on the plant life in the area. You may also want to consider other factors, like wind shelter, campsite traffic flow, and a view. You may also want to place your kitchen well away from your bedroom which brings us to . . .

Camping with Critters

Particularly in bear country, rule number one is: Don't look like, act like, taste like, or smell like food. How do you put it in practice? In your efforts not to be a direct food source for your ursine friends, not only do you want to sleep well away from the kitchen, you should also avoid having food-like smells in your tent. This includes toiletries as well as a tent-mate with hot chocolate on their fleece vest. In places like Alaska, where bears are a real concern, you may want to consider packing a separate set of base layers to act as pj's to sleep in. That way you can keep the clothes that you cooked and ate in stashed with the foodstuffs rather than having them act as a dinner bell in your tent for a hungry grizzly.

You might think that bears, raccoons, and ground squirrels are the main thieves you need to be concerned with, but it all depends on where you are. It could be crows, ravens, the occasional eagle—or in the Caribbean, you could have iguanas or even crabs. In any case, do not feed the animals or become feed yourself.

Chapter 6

BACKWOODS BAKING

T HE ALLURE OF HOT baked goods fresh out of the oven is universal, but when translated to the outdoors it can be downright transcendent. In the last few years much attention has been given to new gadgets to help people bake biscuits, brownies, and even apple pie in the backcountry—where something chocolaty and steaming can mean the difference between a miserable storm and an easily shrugged off shower.

Baking Tips

The learning curve associated with baking in the wilderness is worth every effort and will make you a hero on good days and a deity on tough ones. Following are some general tips to help make your baking success come sooner rather than later:

- Insulate the top of the pan with a dry camp towel (a damp towel will burn you).
- Level the stove using wood or stone chips (put a drop of water into a pan to test).
- Use silicone mitts or dry towels to manipulate a hot oven.
- Never use a damp towel or mitt as a hot pad . . . the resulting steam will burn you.
- For even baking be vigilant and rotate the oven every six to eight minutes.

- Use very low heat. It is better to wait longer than to burn the goods.
- Let smell be your guide. It will smell dryer and sweet when done.
- Sweeter items burn more easily. Remember to use low heat.
- Use a rigid foil windscreen to retain heat around the pan.
- Use a heat diffuser plate to avoid burning.

Choosing a Camp Oven

Over the last two decades I have used a variety of baking devices on sea kayak, canoe, and backpacking trips in different environments. I have also participated in some field tests for magazines. What follows is an evaluation of the relative merits of the products that have stood the test of time. For those of you who prefer a Fred Flintstone approach to technology, I do look at a few low-cost retro-oven ideas that work quite well.

The Outback Oven, the BakePacker and Woody's aluminum Dutch oven were subjected to rigorous trials by several guides in Abel Tasman National Park on the south island of New Zealand as part of a field test for *Sea Kayaker Magazine*. We used baking mixes from bake ware manufacturers, supermarket box mixes, and our own homemade creations. In all cases we judged the baking device's performance by using stoves that supplied heat from one burner underneath the pan.

As in most wilderness areas today, fires were not allowed in Abel Tasman, so we couldn't use hot coals. We didn't need them. There were no failures, and some of the guides may have ascended to guru status after turning out such goodies as crispy baked Camembert cheese and chocolate cakes piped with fresh-whipped cream and strawberries. Our guests never complained about the results of our field trials and were happy to volunteer for further research.

The Outback Oven

Although this is one of the more expensive stovetop camp ovens available, The Outback Oven is one of the best engineered. We tested the model with all the bells and whistles. This compact, little mesh-bagged package consists of a nonstick frying pan without a handle, a heat diffuser, a pot grab, a lid with a heat gauge, a bamboo do-it-all tool, an insulated silver tutu, a heat reflector, and a handy plastic cutting board. Sorry, no Ginsu knives included. It makes quite a light and neat package.

Yes, it is a lot of pieces and gadgets, but when put together the Outback Oven does a great job on cakes, pies, brownies, and pizza. The bottom pan doubles as a good frying pan and the whole unit is fuel-efficient. To use it, the silver tutu rests on the lid and works by convection, collecting heat and funneling it downward providing consistent baking conditions. Your scones won't exactly get golden brown, but they do bake evenly. Plan on a baking time that is five to ten minutes shorter than the average box mix. In fact, if you turn your stove up much past simmer, your brownies will be bricks. So, if your stove only has two speeds—off and blowtorch—you can start that brick fireplace you've always wanted.

On the down side, you do have to take special care of the nonstick coating. Even if you use bamboo or plastic utensils, the coating will scratch simply due to nesting everything together. Try putting the coated half in a plastic bag before packaging it up for travel.

(Source: The Backpackers Pantry at www.backpackerspantry.com)

The BakePacker

We tested the larger model that is designed to fit into the bottom of an 8-inch pot with a bit of skepticism. It was not easy to visualize the end result while looking at a round aluminum waffle. Follow the directions. It works. The ring-shaped aluminum grid suspends whatever you are baking over an inch of boiling water. You simply pour the batter or dough into a durable plastic bag, seal it loosely, nestle it onto the ring, and let the high temperature of steam do the baking. With a tight-fitting lid, you will have enough hot water when you are done to make a cup of coffee to go with your cake. The BakePacker grid doubles as a cake cooling rack or a good place to rest your cooking pot if you don't want to set it in the sand.

If presentation is important to you, be warned: this baby bakes ugly. Once your creation cools enough to extract from the pot, it takes a bit of care to peel off the plastic bag with a minimum amount of destruction. We found wide-diameter bags worked best because we could roll back the edges and invert it to get the dessert to come free. But it still looked like clothes we had slept in. Don't panic, you can work wonders with powdered sugar, whipped cream, or sliced fresh fruit.

The BakePacker works best with sweets due to the very moist goodies it produces, however it does come with a useful no-frills cookbook of its own. This baking device also baked more rapidly than recommended cook times.

(Source: http://www.bakepacker.com)

The Woody

Although the nine-pound aluminum Woody is too heavy to easily carry in a backpack, it bakes amazingly well on a single burner. Its nine-inch-square shape might seem to be an odd package, but it lends itself well to packing and food portioning. The two halves nest into one another and it is well seasoned from the get-go. For best results, make sure the stove is level and place a flexible foil windscreen around the pan and stove.

To bake effectively with the Woody, preheat the unit with its lid on. While preheating the pan for six to eight minutes on medium heat, you can be mixing up whatever you plan to bake—perhaps Jalapeno-Cheddar Cornbread is on the menu to accompany tonight's chili. Simply mix the batter in the zip-seal plastic bag containing the dry mix and squeeze the batter into the waiting hot oven. Turn the heat down to a low simmer, make sure the lid is on tight, and insulate the lid with a couple of small camp towels. You will want to rotate the pan with a pair of mitts and follow your nose. When the bread starts to smell good and "dry", shut off the heat and let it sit a bit to finish. Remove the lid to reveal a golden square of delicious hot bread that will cut beautifully into nine pieces.

You can get similar results with quick breads, brownies, and cakes. If properly insulated and wind-sheltered, you will use very little fuel and your goodies will bake quicker than they would at home.

Banks Fry-Bake Pans

Developed by former NOLS instructor Pam Banks and her father, the Fry-Bake pan is a versatile and quality piece of equipment. It is a hard-anodized aluminum product, much like the most expensive home cookware. It is fairly nonstick and is easily cleaned. The Fry-Bake Pan comes in two sizes; both work well as a frying pan and an oven. Their lids are designed to hold a few coals for a small twig fire. If you are in an area where you can't have a fire, you can cover the lid with a small hand towel to retain the heat and use a heat diffuser plate underneath the pan to keep things from burning. As long as you have a stove that you can adjust to simmer, you should be able to bake cakes, brownies, and quick breads on a single burner.

Retro-Ovens

There are many simple baking methods for the outdoors, ranging from hot coals and palm leaves to ovens fashioned from riverbank clay. There are as many options as there are cultures in the world; here are a couple that I have tried with success.

The Coffee Can Oven—described in the book *One Pan Gourmet,* this is a very simple oven you can make from a three-pound coffee can or a #10 tin salvaged from a local restaurant. To use the can, your small baking pan is suspended above the heat on a rack made of tent pegs skewered through the can. With the right configuration of vent holes and rack heights, the coffee can makes a neat convection oven that doubles as a container for your stove and cook pot. It has a couple of drawbacks, though: it is unstable on a stove due to its top-heavy nature and it can only bake enough for a couple people. You may be able to bake two things at once on two levels. It certainly is an idea worthy of further experimentation.

The Aluminum Ring Mold Oven—is simply a Bundt cake pan or a Jell-O mold with a domed cover. Secondhand shops are usually loaded with them. A small stainless steel bowl makes a good lid and encourages even baking. The greased and battered ring mold is centered over the stove burner so that the heat rises through the hole like a chimney, hits the lid, and rolls down the sides by convection. It is a weird item to pack, but it bakes nice shortcake, biscuits, brownies, and terrific cornbread—as long as you keep the heat very low.

A Final Note

No matter what device you choose, experiment in the backyard to ensure against embarrassing failures in front of ravenous clients and friends. Again, low heat is usually the key to tasty desserts and fresh breads that will evoke Pavlovian responses in the most stoic of campers. Be prepared to handle fame. Being a baking magician during your outdoor exploits can get your presence requested on many adventures. You may have to quit your day job.

Chapter 7

COFFEE AND
OTHER HOT DRINKS

A RGUABLY, THERE IS nothing like a good hot drink on a drizzly day, be it a rich, dark mug of steaming coffee in the morning or a cup of cinnamon-laced Mexican cocoa in the evening. Likewise, a hot cup of tea is more than a mood lifter—it can be a lifesaver on a cold day. In a way, it is all medicinal and it is all good.

Coffee

For many people, coffee is serious business. Without it, they can't start their day. Caffeine addicts enjoy the brew in many different ways, and your excursion will be much better if proper planning and research is done about your travel partner's tastes.

The Ground Rules
- The cook gets the first cup and nobody gets hurt.
- Strong coffee can easily be diluted, but not vice versa.
- Good beans make good coffee.
- Vacation time is too short for bad brew.
- Instant coffee is for emergencies only.

Brewing Methods: It's a Personal Taste
French Press: This makes a good cup of joe as long as you don't

grind the beans too finely. Insulated plastic presses are available, as are Lexan models that are fragile if unprotected.

Percolator: This makes rich, uniquely flavored nostalgic brew. The pot can be used as a tea kettle and will boil noodles, otherwise it is a fairly useless container. It takes a while to make and you only get coffee from that one pot simmering away.

Filter Drip: Essentially it works the same as a standard electric coffeemaker by dripping hot water over your waiting ground coffee nested in a filter funnel perched on a mug or thermal bottle. It makes great coffee since the water is truly hot enough and it is simple. This method has some big advantages. Since you start breakfast by boiling water in your largest pot, you will have enough water to use for tea, cocoa, boiled eggs, oatmeal, etc., and still have some to pour over your favorite coffee blend. I use a large funnel that sits atop a thermos (pre-warmed with boiling water) to produce nearly limitless coffee for large groups and java sponges. Any leftover coffee is already

> It seems like you can't travel for more than an hour in New Zealand before you have to halt for a "cuppa."

packaged to travel in the thermos. For clean-up, you dry the moisture out of the wet grounds and filters before packing out or use a reusable hemp cloth filter.

Perfect Cowboy Coffee: There is an art to this and it produces some pretty tasty java. There are lots of ways to make cowboy coffee; this is mine: Pour cold water into your brewing pot and add roughly one tablespoon of ground coffee per cup of water; bring to a boil. Turn off the heat as soon as it starts to boil; stir a bit and let stand for a couple of minutes. Here's the trick: put a few drops of cold drinking water into the pot and tap on the side of the pot for a few seconds with a fork to get the grounds to settle to the bottom. Slowly pour the liquid into your mug and enjoy. It is fun and really good.

> Any remaining hot water from your drink-making routine can be put in a flask to warm the foot of your sleeping bag. In the morning, you will have drinking water near at hand.

Espresso: My dear friend Nigel has traveled with his portable espresso kit all over the world for more than a decade. He has a fine-tuned system and if he has three minutes to spare, he will brew a shot. Having enjoyed many espressos with Nigel, I have to say it is a great system. He carries a nifty stovetop espresso maker and brews atop a tiny butane stove.

In fact, you can purchase these espresso makers, stoves, and lovely Kri Kri designed espresso tumblers by following the online store links at www.nigelkayaks.com.

Tea: There is no such thing as too much of this comfort brew on a trip. Know your crew, though, as someone might spring that dreaded question: Do you have any Rooibos Vanilla Soy Chai Latte with raw honey?

Hot Cocoa: Chocolate is safety gear, i.e., if you forget to pack it your life could be in danger. Buy the best instant hot chocolate you can find and mix it with a bit of instant creamer or dried whole milk for a really rich cup that will keep you and your crew warm on a cold evening.

Coffee and Other Hot Drinks

Cabbage is Immortal

One late August I noticed an unusually unpleasant odor wafting out of the front hatch of my sea kayak. Not yesterday's-socks unpleasant—but truly something to attract circling vultures. The kayak also seemed a bit bow heavy when I carried it single-handedly. Nothing rattled when I shook it, but when I stood it hard on its tail, there was a sickening flump against the front bulkhead.

I gradually worked up my courage and peeked inside the reeking darkness, where I discovered a slimy purplish lump. Scooping it out with my paw, I recognized the remains of a red cabbage that had been lodged there since June. Even the Kraut Festival across the Big Lake in Franksville, Wisconsin, would have rejected it. But, oddly enough, after I sloughed off a few layers, it still made an excellent salad that evening!

Chapter 8

PORTABLE PRODUCE

MANY EXPLORERS LAUNCHING a multi-day trip face a diet of nondescript sawdust in foil packets. Lightweight foods engineered for backcountry travel lose a lot of flavor and nutrients during processing. They also acquire a texture that is best described as *glop*. Gone is any crispness that is associated with fresh fruits and vegetables. It seems that when spending valuable and limited vacation time on a dream trip, we provision ourselves as if we are mounting a three-month polar journey. Of course, on backpacking trips and paddling outings that involve portages weight is at a premium. In those cases, food with most of the water removed is more practical. On the other hand, if you are on a paddling or a raft trip where weight isn't a big issue, you might as well enjoy the fresh stuff. With careful planning you can take a large variety of fresh produce for seven or eight days and not miss any of the wonderful crunchiness that tells your mouth to "Wake up!"

Imagine yourself three days into a summer kayak tour. You've just put in a fifteen-mile day in a stiff headwind and carried your gear across a mid-tide mudflat. As the sun starts to droop towards the horizon, you begin to fantasize about a nice glass of wine, a crisp Caesar salad, angel hair pasta with shrimp in a lime-garlic sauce, followed by a warm chewy brownie and a hot steaming cup of coffee laced with Irish cream . . .

But wait, those are real aromas coming from the cook zone. This meal is really going to happen—right here, right now! This group knows how to enjoy their time off.

So, how do you travel with fresh produce without it looking and smelling like something the tide left on the beach?

Avoid Death by Suffocation

Our nutrient-laden friends need air to survive. Various sizes of mesh bags (like the ones used for oranges, grapefruit, and onions) do a fantastic job at preserving a variety of fruits and vegetables. You will be amazed at how well things keep—even at warm temperatures. Certain fruits need a little tenderness though—bananas, apples, grapes, avocados, and tomatoes. Not only do they need air but they also require a rigid container to protect their fragile hides. One way to create safe havens for these items is to collect a variety of rigid re-sealable containers, slip into a testosterone frenzy and drill 'em full of small holes . . . all in the quest of tenderness, of course. Reusing plastic ice-cream tubs works well for this because when they are empty they can easily be nested. Some fruit, like melons, can be chilled by sinking them in deep water in a dunk bag weighted down with rocks, a bottle of wine, and maybe some heavy cream to be whipped later as an addition to strawberry shortcake.

Shady Characters

In camp you can avoid contact with the ground and small critters by hanging your produce in the shade under a tree. If you are traveling by canoe or kayak, nestle your most perishable items below the waterline against the hull and cover with other insulating layers, like raingear or sleeping pads (not recommended for bear country, however). This is a very cool, dark, place to keep produce—not unlike the vegetable drawer in your fridge (okay, maybe it's even cleaner).

Life Expectancy

We have become used to having every convenience at out fingertips; we tend to forget that people thrived before frost-free refrigerators and microwave ovens. In fact, many of the items we refrigerate today can survive and thrive without the big chill. This is especially true for many fruits and vegetables, some of which even taste better if kept at room temperature.

The following is a list of fruits and vegetables that can travel with you in the wilderness and their life expectancies. Extreme cold or extreme heat will greatly affect these time estimates, but there are always ways to cheat.

Vegetables

Avocados: 2 to 4 days depending on ripeness at outset

Beets: 4 to 8 days

Bell peppers: up to 7 days

Carrots, whole and unpeeled: 4 to 8 days

Chinese or celery cabbage: 3 to 5 days

Red or Green cabbage: immortal (see page 35)

Cucumbers: 1 to 4 days with no punctures or bruising

Eggplant: 3 to 4 days

Garlic, Fresh: 2 to 4 weeks

Mushrooms, Fresh: turn to slime in 2 to 3 days, dried varieties work best

Onions: 2 to 4 weeks

Potatoes, red, white, or sweet: up to a month

Romaine lettuce: 4 days in a "cheater pack" cooler

Summer or Zucchini squash: 2 to 4 days

Fresh Fruits

Apples, firm variety, like Granny Smith: 7+ days if they don't get bruised

Bananas: 3 to 7 days if they are not abused

Blueberries: 1 to 3 days

Cantaloupe: 2 to 5 days depending on ripeness at outset

Citrus (grapefruit, lemons, limes, oranges): 1 to 2 weeks

Grapes, green and red: 2 to 3 days

Kiwi: 2 to 4 days if they don't get bruised

Peaches: you wish!

Pineapples: 2 to 5 days depending on ripeness at outset

Plums: 2 to 6 days

Tomatoes: 2 to 5 days

COOKING SECRETS AND TIPS

- Pack a good spice kit.

- Remember your favorite sauces.

- Fresh herbs make food taste fresher and they are quite portable. Wrap uncut herbs in a damp paper towel and then package them loosely in a cellophane-lined paper coffee bag (the type you buy coffee beans in). The herbs will keep this way for a few days; even longer if stashed in the top of a soft-sided cooler.

- Kitchen shears work very well to cut sun-dried tomatoes.

- Heat management: use a heat diffuser plate on the stove burner to avoid burning and a foil windscreen to retain heat underneath pots and pans.

- Small micro-fiber kitchen towels are lightweight, easy to clean, and work as hot pads, top insulators, napkins, placemats, and even . . . well . . . towels.

- Wine adds nice flavor to a number of dishes and is available in small Tetra Pak containers or Mylar® bags inside of paperboard boxes. Leave the box behind and you have an easy-to-stow package of wine. Generally speaking, the quality of the wine decreases as the size of the container increases.

- Devise a flexible plan before your departure and your entire backcountry experience will go better; not just your meals.

Miles Per Pancake

For his 80th birthday, Verlen Kruger, one of the greatest paddling legends of our time, paddled the full length of the Yukon River with his wife, Jenny—all 2,300 miles—in 80 days. From the age of 40, when he took up paddling, to 80, when he passed away, he logged well over 100,000 miles in decked canoes of his own design. His secret? Pancakes.

For his honeymoon (one of), Verlen and Valerie Fons shared a little paddle from the top of North America to the bottom of South America—26,500 or so miles in about three years. That was slightly shorter than the trip Verlen took a few years earlier. To crank out that kind of mileage, he didn't like to stop to cook or sleep more than he had to. He pretty much tried to "eat and paddle, eat and paddle." This is how he did it. When he stopped, he cooked pancakes … a lot of pancakes. After they cooled, he packed them four to a bag and stuffed them next to the seat hangars in his Sea Wind decked canoe. Then, when he was paddling and felt a hunger pang, he simply munched on a pancake between strokes … for days.

Verlen swore he got four miles to a pancake.

PART TWO

Let's Cook!

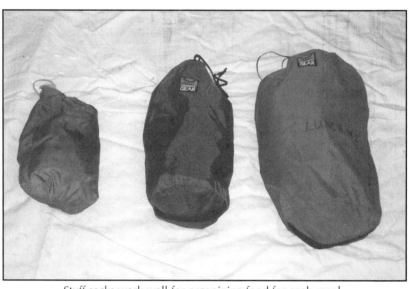

Stuff sacks work well for organizing food for each meal.

Chapter 9

BREAKFAST

S KIPPING THE FIRST meal of the day when you are engaged in active pursuits is not productive. You need fuel for energy and, depending on the season, possibly for warmth. Light and fast packers as well as some winter campers will often develop a high powered breakfast product that they consume daily as fuel for both energy and warmth. While food is certainly fuel, a tasty and satisfying breakfast sets the tone for a great day. The fare can be as simple as a boiled egg, freshly roasted coffee, and a great hot cereal—or as elaborate as Eggs Benedict.

The flavor and enjoyment of any breakfast is greatly enhanced when you are perched on a large rock feeling the morning rays of the sun warming you and sending sparkles across the water next to camp.

The recipes that follow start out fast and simple and work toward more sophisticated meals—which are still deceptively easy to prepare.

At Home Preparations

Pack eggs (in their shells) so they don't break. An ideal container is rigid, like a wide-mouthed water bottle or a reused plastic peanut butter jar. Never break eggs into a container first, unless you enjoy food poisoning as a weight-loss method. Pour ground coffee or pancake mix or instant dry milk in the container so that it fills the voids around the eggs. This keeps the eggs intact for backpacking. For paddling trips, Styrofoam egg containers sealed with a round of duct tape work just fine.

SIMPLE 10-MINUTE 3-COURSE BREAKFAST

Here is a favorite quick-and-easy breakfast that works just about any-where. And one pot yields three hot items in a short amount of time. Genius!

AT HOME

Pack eggs in their shell in a rigid container like a wide-mouthed water bottle or a re-used peanut butter jar. Add ground coffee (or oats, pancake mix, etc) to fill all the voids around the eggs. This will keeps eggs intact for backpacking while we've found that foam egg boxes sealed with a round of duct take work great for paddling trips.

IN CAMP

Fill a pot with water and gently lower eggs into the water. Bring water and eggs to a gentle boil. Remove eggs after desired boiling time (4 minutes for soft, 5 for semi-soft, 8 for hard-boiled). Next pour boiling water to make your choice of hot beverage (water is clean if the eggs did not crack). Add your choice of hot cereal to remaining water and simmer till done.

This meal provides a nice combination of complex carbohydrates from the hot cereal and a shot of protein from the egg. Your choices for hot cereal are nearly limitless—oats, muesli, granola, 7-grain, and a few good recipes that follow. Let the eggs cool while you sip your mug of hot coffee or tea.

Shopping List:	Number of Campers			
	2	4	6	12
Cereal	2 c	4 c	6 c	12 c
Eggs	2	4	6	12
SWEETENERS:				
Honey	1 T	2 T	3 T	½ c
Brown Sugar	1 T	2 T	3 T	½ c
Maple Syrup	1 T	2 T	3 T	½ c

VARIATIONS AND COMMENTS

If you like flavored coffee, lace the coffee grounds with a few dashes of ground cinnamon before pouring in the water. If you encounter wild blueberries or raspberries toss them into the cereal while cooking it for a tasty treat. If you have leftover cooked cereal, blend it into a batch of pancake batter the next day for hotcakes that pack a little more punch.

KIWI MUESLI

Traditionally a European breakfast staple, this recipe was given to me by a friend from New Zealand; it is a great improvement on the original.

AT HOME

Put rolled oats in a large microwave-safe bowl and zap on high in the microwave for three minutes. Stir and repeat three times until oats are hot and a bit toasted smelling (you may want to reduce the time to two-minute intervals for smaller amounts of oats and/or powerful microwaves). Drizzle the brown sugar and honey on the heated oats; stir to coat uniformly. Toss in the nuts, pumpkin-seeds, and finely grated coconut. Return bowl to microwave and heat on high for 2 to 3 minutes. Stir and repeat four times. This will toast the nuts and dry the sweeteners into the oats. Remove from microwave. Stir in the remaining dried fruit bits. Let cool. Bag in zip-seal bags and store in freezer until ready to use or pack up for a trip. This muesli is a tasty breakfast staple, so quantities start at six servings.

IN CAMP

Simply eat by the handful or add powdered or evaporated milk, soy or spiced-cider mix, or prepare the muesli as a hot cereal. In this latter category, it will please even those who dislike oatmeal.

Shopping List:	Number of Campers		
	6	12	18
Oats, rolled	3 c	6 c	9 c
Coconut (unsweetened, finely shredded)	½ c	1 c	1½ c
Walnuts, pieces	1 c	2 c	3 c
Pumpkin seeds, shelled and unsalted	½ c	1 c	1½ c
Raisins	½ c	1 c	1½ c
Dried Cherries	½ c	1 c	1½ c
Dried Apricots (chopped)	½ c	1 c	1½ c
SWEETENERS:			
Honey	1 T	2 T	3 T
Brown Sugar	1 T	2 T	3 T

B
R
E
A
K
F
A
S
T

VARIATIONS AND COMMENTS

You can use any combination of dried fruit or nuts you like; the above combination is my favorite. The dried apricots provide an amazing taste explosion in this cereal. If you want to try this at home in true Bavarian style, simply put a cup of muesli in a bowl, cover it with apple cider or apple juice and refrigerate or simply soak overnight. Serve with a dollop of vanilla yogurt and sliced apple on top. I know it sounds impossibly healthy, but it tastes so good you will forget that it is good for you.

KATHLEEN'S CHERRY-NUT GRANOLA

Contributed by my office manager, Kathleen, this crunchy cereal is noisier than eating Cap'n Crunch. It is a favorite at our Greenland-style kayak-training camp. This makes a great trail snack, base for GORP, hot or cold cereal.

AT HOME

Make a large quantity of this cereal and consider buying your ingredients from bulk bins at a supermarket or food co-op to get exactly the quantities you need—it is far less expensive that way. It is a bit labor-intensive, but the results are well worth it.

Mix all dry ingredients together and toast in a 300° F oven in cake pans for 15 minutes to pre-warm. Mix all wet ingredients together; stir into the dry mixture until coated. Continue roasting in oven at 300° F; stir well every 20 minutes until liquids have turned to a crunchy glaze. Add dried cherries last. After it has cooled, divide into one-pound portions in zip-seal bags.

IN CAMP

Snack right from the bag or cook with twice the water as a hot cereal.

Shopping List:	Number of Campers		
	6	12	18
DRY INGREDIENTS:			
Oats, rolled	1½ c	3 c	5 c
Wheat Flakes	1½ c	3 c	5 c
Walnuts, pieces	1 c	2 c	2½ c
Almonds, sliced or slivered	1 c	2 c	2½ c
Pecans	1 c	2 c	2½ c
Sunflower Seeds (unsalted)	½ c	1c	1½ c
Dried Cherries	1 lb	1½ lbs	2 lbs
SWEETENERS:			
Honey	½ c	1 c	1½ c
Oil (Canola or Peanut)	1/3 c	2/3 c	1 c
Vanilla Extract	1 t	2 t	1 T

B R E A K F A S T *(vertical marginal tab)*

VARIATIONS AND COMMENTS

Customize the mix by adding nuts and fruits to your personal taste. Be aware of nut allergies among your fellow campers.

HUEVOS RANCHEROS

This is a great way to recycle leftover veggie chili into a breakfast that will power you until four p.m.

AT HOME
Pack three or four extra eggs than what this recipe requires. Extra eggs can be boiled at breakfast for a snack or an addition to the lunch menu.

IN CAMP
Prep time: 20 minutes / one pan, one pot

After dinner on chili night, put the leftovers in a re-sealable plastic bag and store the bag in your cheater pack or lay it flat on the floor inside a cool, sealed kayak hatch. In the morning, heat leftover chili on low heat in a small pot or drop the sealed bag into leftover hot coffee water to heat slowly while you cook the eggs.

Fry eggs to order in pan, top with a scoop of hot chili, a sprinkle of cheddar cheese, and a dollop of salsa. Serve with flour tortillas toasted in the egg pan.

Shopping List:	Number of Campers			
	2	4	6	12
Eggs	4	6	12	24
Cheddar Cheese	2 oz	4 oz	6 oz	12 oz
Salsa	2 oz	3 oz	4 oz	8 oz
Flour Tortillas, 8-inch	4	8	12	24

B
R
E
A
K
F
A
S
T

VARIATIONS AND COMMENTS
I like to use the small tins (2 to 4 ounces) of Mexican salsa you can find in the international section of most supermarkets. The salsa can also be dried into salsa leather if you are packing for a lightweight trip. Likewise, dried egg substitute can be used instead of fresh eggs. These can be improved greatly by putting the cheese and salsa right in the eggs.

Yup, it is as good as any you'll eat anywhere—and it is really easy!

JAMIE'S EGGS DURANGO

Jamie Jackson brings us this recipe from Durango, Colorado. He runs kayak tours in Key Largo and markets a hardy sailor's rum from the Virgin Islands called Pusser's. It's a fast and easy meal to prepare that stretches small amounts of eggs.

AT HOME

Pre-shred the cheese and package it in a re-sealable plastic bag. Package whole eggs so they won't break (never break them into a container for travel, unless you enjoy food poisoning).

IN CAMP

Prep time: 10 minutes / one frying pan

Heat a small amount of olive oil in the bottom of a frying pan. Beat eggs with a little water until foamy; add to hot pan, scrambling until half set. Add cheese, tortilla chips, and salsa. Keep stirring until cheese is melted, eggs are set, and chips are half-crunchy. Great way to use smashed chips—and the more chips you add, the more the eggs grow! Actually works well with Frito's corn chips.

Shopping List:	Number of Campers			
	2	4	6	12
Eggs	3	6	9	18
Tortilla Chips	1 oz	2 oz	3 oz	6 oz
Cheese (anything you like)	1 oz	2 oz	3 oz	6 oz
Salsa (more if you like it hotter)	1 oz	2 oz	3 oz	6 oz

HERBS AND SPICES:
Black Pepper, to taste
Cumin, to taste

VARIATIONS AND COMMENTS

Instead of tortilla chips you can use leftover tortillas, simply tear them into bite-size pieces. Feel free to add leftover chili, veggies, corn—whatever you like. Remember, the beauty of this recipe is its simplicity.

B
R
E
A
K
F
A
S
T

48

ENCHILADA SCRAMBLE

This one is hearty and delicious, although a bit on the ugly side. You will have to get over its appearance because it is tasty. I make this at home by scrambling leftover enchiladas into eggs, but this "trail version" is even better.

AT HOME
Pack three or four extra eggs than what this recipe calls requires. Extra eggs can be boiled at breakfast for a snack or an addition to the lunch menu. Store chunk cheese in a re-sealable bag and package veggies so they can breathe.

IN CAMP
Prep time: 20 minutes / one pan

Sauté chopped onions, corn (drained), and spices in a little olive oil. Add shredded corn tortillas. Stir in beaten eggs, salsa, and diced green chilies. (Canned green chilies have great flavor, but are not hot.) Scramble until almost cooked, then add chopped or grated cheddar cheese and finish cooking. Serve on flour tortillas as breakfast burritos or just heap in separate bowls.

Shopping List:	Number of Campers			
	2	**4**	**6**	**12**
Eggs	4	6	12	24
Onion, small	½	1	1½	3
Corn, canned, drained	4 oz	8 oz	12 oz	24 oz
Cheddar Cheese	2 oz	4 oz	6 oz	12 oz
Green Chilies, 4 oz. can	1	1	2	3
Corn Tortillas	2	3	6	12
Salsa	2 oz	3 oz	4 oz	8 oz
Flour Tortillas, 12-inch	6	12	18	36
HERBS AND SPICES:				
Cumin	pinch	¼ t	½ t	1 t
Chili Powder	½ t	¾ t	1 t	2 t
Black Pepper, to taste				
Bottled Pepper Sauce for an extra kick				

VARIATIONS AND COMMENTS
You can substitute an 8 oz. can of tomato sauce for the salsa if you double the chili powder.

B
R
E
A
K
F
A
S
T

BREAKFAST TACOS

This power food packs a punch until lunch and beyond.

AT HOME

Pack a few extra eggs than what this recipe requires. Extra eggs can be boiled at breakfast for a snack or an addition to the lunch menu. Store chunk cheese in a re-sealable plastic bag and package veggies so they can breathe.

IN CAMP

Prep time: 20 minutes / one pan

Finely chop red potatoes, onions, and bell pepper; sauté in olive oil on medium flame until spuds are tender. Sprinkle with cumin and pepper; stir. Add beaten eggs. Scramble until almost cooked; then add chopped or grated cheddar cheese. Stir until finished cooking. Fold egg mixture onto small flour tortillas and top with salsa. You can warm tortillas atop the eggs with a good cover after you've turned off the heat.

Shopping List:	Number of Campers			
	2	**4**	**6**	**12**
Eggs	4	8	12	24
Red Potatoes, small	2	4	6	12
Onion, small	½	1	1½	3
Bell Pepper	½	1	1½	3
Cheddar Cheese	2 oz	4 oz	6 oz	12 oz
Flour Tortillas, 8-inch	6	12	18	36
HERBS AND SPICES:				
Cumin	pinch	¼ t	½ t	1 t
Black Pepper, to taste				
Salsa for topping				

B

R

E

A

K

F

A

S

T

VARIATIONS AND COMMENTS

For a richer-tasting and low-fat alternative substitute light cream cheese (Neufchatel) for the cheddar cheese. For a lightweight version, you can also substitute dried egg replacer and dry hash browns for the red skins. Just soak the hash browns in cold water for thirty minutes first, drain, and pre-brown a bit before adding other ingredients. Try adding canned or freeze-dried corn to the egg mixture along with dried coriander. Chili powder and canned diced green chilies are also good additives. Do you get the idea that this is a hard recipe to mess up?

FARMER'S OMELET FRITTATA

This is simple, hearty and I have made it in large enough quantities to feed forty people—to rave reviews.

AT HOME
Store chunk cheese in a re-sealable plastic bag.

IN CAMP
Prep time: 50 minutes / one pan

In the bottom of a Dutch oven brown the onion and thawed hash browns (or re-hydrated dried) in olive oil. This can be done in a hot oven in the bottom of a baking pan as well. Cover with a layer of shredded cheddar cheese and cubed ham or Canadian-style bacon. Pour beaten eggs over this mixture, sprinkle a bit more cheddar cheese on top, and cover. Bake for 30 to 40 minutes until set.

Shopping List:	Number of Campers			
	2	4	6	12
Eggs	4	6	10	18
Hash Browns, frozen OR	8 oz	12 oz	16 oz	2 lbs
Hash Browns, dried	2 oz	4 oz	6 oz	12 oz
Onion, chopped	½ c	1 c	1½ c	3 c
Sharp Cheddar Cheese, shredded	½ c	¾ c	1 c	2 c
Smoked Ham, cubed in small pieces	½ c	¾ c	1 c	2 c

HERBS AND SPICES:
Salt and Pepper to taste

VARIATIONS AND COMMENTS
This meal is more likely to be made and served at home as a hearty brunch dish. It is great for a large group of people.

VEGGIE FRITTATA

The combination of Italian herbs and vegetables makes this a crowd pleaser.

AT HOME

Package veggies so they can breathe.

IN CAMP

Prep time: 50 minutes / one Dutch oven, one frying pan

In a frying pan, sauté assorted vegetables, herbs, and garlic in a little olive oil for a few minutes to marry the flavors together. While the veggies are cooking, lay out bread slices (French or pretty much anything will do) in a single layer on bottom of oiled baking pan or Dutch oven. Stack ham, salami, or turkey slices along with sliced provolone cheese on bread. Pour vegetable mixture over this and cover with beaten eggs. Top with shredded Parmesan cheese and bake for 30 to 40 minutes until set. This smells incredible as it is baking.

Shopping List:	Number of Campers			
	2	4	6	12
Eggs, beaten	4	6	10	18
Bread, slices	2	4	4	8
Onion, small	½	1	1½	3
Red Bell Pepper	½	1	1½	3
Zucchini (sliced)	½ c	1 c	1 c	2 c
Fresh Mushrooms (sliced)	½ c	1 c	1 c	2 c
Broccoli, pieces	½ c	1 c	1 c	2 c
Parmesan Cheese, grated	2 T	¼ c	¼ c	½ c
Deli Meat and Cheese	Enough to top each slice of bread in a single layer			
HERBS AND SPICES:				
Mixed Italian Herbs	½ t	¾ t	1 t	2 t
Salt and Pepper, to taste				

B

R

E

A

K

F

A

S

T

VARIATIONS AND COMMENTS

You can use just about any vegetable, cheese, or sliced meat for this meal. These were chosen for an Italian accent. You could easily give it a Greek flavor with spinach, feta and ripe juicy olives. The amounts for four and six people are virtually the same because this recipe makes a lot. Actually, it is tough to make just two servings, so be prepared to use the leftovers later. Although this recipe works well in a Dutch oven, you can easily prepare and serve this at home as a hearty brunch dish.

ORANGE RUM RAISIN FRENCH TOAST

This recipe might sound involved, but it is actually easy and yields a flavorful hot meal that you will want to serve at home on special Sunday mornings.

AT HOME
Be sure your spice kit is packed with the right stuff for this one.

IN CAMP
Prep time: 25 minutes / one pan, one bowl

Beat eggs in a bowl. Stir in evaporated milk, grated orange peel, juice from your fresh orange, nutmeg, cinnamon, and real vanilla extract. You may want to thicken the batter slightly by adding a small amount of pancake flour that has been mixed with a bit of water to form a paste—it helps coat the bread. Dip thick-sliced raisin bread into batter (bakery bread works best) and coat thoroughly before browning on both sides in a frying pan. Serve with maple syrup, dust with confectioner's sugar, or top with fresh fruit and yogurt.

Shopping List:	Number of Campers			
	2	4	6	12
Eggs	2	4	6	12
Raisin Bread (loaf)	½	1	1½	3
Oranges, for juice and peel	1	1	1	3
Orange Peel, grated	1 t	1½ t	2 t	1 T
Evaporated Milk (small can)	1	1	2	4
SPICES:				
Vanilla Extract, real	1 t	1½ t	2 t	1 T
Ground Nutmeg	¼ t	½ t	¾ t	1½ t
Cinnamon	½ t	1 t	1½ t	1 T
Confectioner's Sugar	a dusting			
Rum	1 T	1½ T	2 T	3 T
Maple Syrup	2 T	4 T	½ c	1 c

VARIATIONS AND COMMENTS
This is basically the same recipe as Backcountry Pain Perdue, but it calls for raisin bread and uses a bit of rum to help keep the spices suspended.

B
R
E
A
K
F
A
S
T

BACKCOUNTRY PAIN PERDUE

Whether you top this with confectioner's sugar or a hot fruit compote, you will feel like you are eating at a fine New Orleans's sidewalk cafe, without the traffic noise and the smell of stale beer.

AT HOME

Duct tape the bag(s) of French bread in the cockpit on the underside of your kayak's deck or to the bottom of your canoe seat.

IN CAMP

Prep time: 20 minutes / one pan, one pot

Beat eggs in a bowl. Stir in evaporated milk, grated orange peel, orange juice, nutmeg, cinnamon, and real vanilla extract. At this point you can add a dash of rum, brandy, or Grand Marnier to bind the flavors and keep the spices in suspension. You may even want to thicken the batter with a small amount of pancake flour mixed with some water to form a paste—it helps coat the bread. Dip thick-sliced French bread into the batter and coat thoroughly before browning on both sides. Serve with maple syrup, dust with confectioner's sugar, or top with a hot fruit compote. This dish looks as beautiful as it tastes.

Shopping List:	Number of Campers			
	2	**4**	**6**	**12**
Eggs	2	4	6	12
French Bread (loaf)	½	1	1½	3
Orange	1	1	2	3
Evaporated Milk (small can)	1	1	2	4
SPICES:				
Vanilla Extract, real	1 t	1½ t	2 t	1 T
Ground Nutmeg	¼ t	½ t	¾ t	1½ t
Cinnamon	½ t	1 t	1½ t	1 T
Confectioner's Sugar	a dusting			
Liquor	1 t	2 t	3 t	2 T
Maple Syrup	2 T	4 T	½ c	1 c

B
R
E
A
K
F
A
S
T

VARIATIONS AND COMMENTS

Hot wild-berry compote is a great topping. Simply cook foraged blueberries, huckleberries, or raspberries with a pinch of cinnamon, a small amount of water, and a few drops of maple syrup to make a thick, delicious, hot topping that is worth the effort. You can also simmer dried cherries (they're pre-sweetened) in an equal amount of water to create a hot sauce that will give your breakfast the feel of hot cherry pie.

BELIZEAN FRYJACKS

I ran into this staple while working with Belizean guides. No getting around it, they are evil. But, when made right, they are delicious and not too greasy.

AT HOME
Package the flour in a zip-seal bag.

IN CAMP
Prep time: 25 minutes / one pan

Put flour and a pinch of salt in a pot. Add the oil. Using a fork, mix until thoroughly blended. While continuing to stir the mixture, add water a bit at a time until you have what resembles bread dough. Lightly oil your hands and knead the dough for about five minutes until it is smooth and elastic. Form a golf-ball sized sphere of dough and put it on an oiled plate. Flatten it with your fingers until it is about 8 inches in diameter. Quarter it with a knife.

Heat a quarter-inch of canola oil in a frying pan. Gently lower the dough quarters into the hot oil. Fry for about one minute, then turn. They should puff up like crazy. When puffed and light brown, remove from the frying pan onto a plate. While these drain, fry the next batch.

Shopping List:	Number of Campers			
	2	4	6	12
Flour	1 c	2 c	3 c	6 c
Canola Oil	1 t	2 t	1 T	2 T

VARIATIONS AND COMMENTS
Fry jacks are great with jam, dusted with sugar, or stuffed with scrambled eggs with cheese and salsa. In Belize, it is common to eat these for breakfast with eggs and refried beans or with a small fried fish called a Jack—in other words, fryjacks with your fried Jack. If you opt for the sweet end of the scale, dust them with cinnamon sugar for a county fair elephant-ear style treat.

B
R
E
A
K
F
A
S
T

FIVE-MILE PANCAKE MIX

You can use a prepared mix if you like. There are some excellent ones but I usually augment them a bit. 10-Grain mix from Bob's Red Mill is commonly available in supermarkets; it produces light, tasty pancakes. I often add egg powder and buttermilk powder to it at home to make it a just-add-water mix for easy backcountry cooking. Or you can prepare this simple mixture at home. I produce five pounds at a time for a basic mix.

AT HOME

Sift together dry ingredients; mix thoroughly. Store in twist-tied bags. Flour clogs zip-sealed bags so that they don't close well.

IN CAMP

Prep time: 15 to 20 minutes / one frying pan or griddle

Combine dry mix with liquids; stir just until big lumps are gone. Hold back a bit of liquid until the end so you can make the batter thinner if desired. Heat a griddle or frying pan on a medium flame until drops of water dance on it. Lightly coat the pan with oil and fry cakes, turning once when edges look done. Serve with hot apple mixture spooned over the top instead of maple syrup—or use both for a real treat.

Shopping List:	Number of Campers			
	2	4	6	12
FIVE-MILE MIX INGREDIENTS				
Flour	1 c	2 c	3 c	6 c
Sugar	1½ t	1 T	1½ T	3 T
Salt	½ t	1 t	1½ t	1 T
Baking Powder	1½ t	1 T	1½ T	3 T
Buttermilk Powder	1 T	2 T	3 T	6 T
TO MAKE IN CAMP				
Dry Mix	1½ c	2½ c	4 c	7 c
Eggs, beaten	1	2	2	4
Oil or Melted Butter	1 T	2 T	2½ T	4 T
Water (or milk)	1 c	1½ c	2 c	4 c
Maple Syrup	2 T	4 T	½ c	1 c

B

R

E

A

K

F

A

S

T

VARIATIONS AND COMMENTS

Add vanilla extract, mashed bananas, wild blueberries, chocolate chips, raspberries, re-hydrated dried cherries, walnuts, or raisins to the batter. I often add a few tablespoons of cornmeal in with the dry mix to give the pancakes a nice texture.

RUDY'S ISLAND PANCAKES

On Roatan Island, Honduras, where I work in the winter, there is a very large black man with a huge beard who owns a café on the West End. Wearing a very large T-shirt with a large picture of himself on it, he welcomes all visitors with his brilliant white smile and the question, "How are you on this beautiful Sunday morning?" He asks this any day of the week at virtually anytime, because it is always sun day on Roatan. He makes these wonderful banana-spice pancakes that are the perfect end to bananas that haven't adapted well to a traveling life.

AT HOME
You can pre-mix the spices in with the pancake mix. Sometimes I will freeze the flesh of over-ripe bananas in a zip-seal plastic bag and then pack them in my soft-sided cooler for use the first or second morning of a trip.

IN CAMP
Prep time: 20 to 25 minutes / one frying pan or griddle

Crush very ripe bananas into a pot, stir in eggs and vanilla extract; beat until it forms a fragrant puree. Add dry pancake mix and water or evaporated milk a little at a time until batter reaches the desired consistency. Heat a frying pan or griddle on a medium flame until drops of water dance on it. Lightly coat the pan with oil and fry the cakes, turning once when edges look done. These pancakes smell incredible when they are cooking—kind of like having warm banana bread for breakfast!

Shopping List:	Number of Campers			
	2	**4**	**6**	**12**
Five-Mile Pancake mix	1½ c	3 c	5 c	8 c
Water or milk	1 c	1½ c	2 c	4 c
Vegetable oil or melted butter	1 T	2 T	2½ T	4 T
Eggs, beaten	1	2	2	4
Bananas	1	2	3	6
SPICES:				
Vanilla Extract, real	1 t	2 t	1 T	2 T
Cinnamon	½ t	1 t	2 t	1 T
Nutmeg	pinch	¼ t	½ t	1 t
Allspice	pinch	¼ t	½ t	1 t
Brown Sugar	2 t	1 T	1½ T	3 T
Maple Syrup	2 T	4 T	½ c	1 c

B
R
E
A
K
F
A
S
T

VARIATIONS AND COMMENTS
These pancakes are very good topped with canned crushed pineapple (drained) or apricot jam.

LEMON POPPY SEED PANCAKES

These fragrant pancakes will remind you of the muffins of the same name, but less sweet.

AT HOME

You can add poppy seeds to the dry pancake mix. Package eggs to travel.

IN CAMP

Prep time: 20 to 25 minutes / one frying pan or griddle

Roll lemons under pressure on the bottom of a pot to make them juicier. Shave off lemon zest with a pocketknife and cut into fine bits. Mix the batter and add lemon zest and juice together. Heat a griddle or frying pan on a medium flame until drops of water dance on it. Lightly coat the pan with oil and fry the cakes, turning once when edges look done.

Shopping List:	Number of Campers			
	2	**4**	**6**	**12**
Five-Mile Pancake Mix	1½ c	3 c	5 c	8 c
Water or milk	1 c	1½ c	2 c	4 c
Vegetable oil or melted butter	1 T	2 T	2½ T	4 T
Eggs, beaten	1	2	2	4
Lemons	1	2	3	5
Lemon Zest (yellow part of peel)	1 T	1½ T	2 T	3 T
Poppy Seeds	1 T	1½ T	2 T	3 T
SPICES:				
Vanilla Extract, real	1 t	2 t	1 T	2 T
Sugar, granulated	2 t	1 T	1½ T	3 T

B R E A K F A S T

VARIATIONS AND COMMENTS

These are delicious with blueberries added to the mix, with powdered sugar sprinkled on top, or turned into a thinner batter and cooked crepe style. If you are making these at home or have access to a cooler, add a half cup of sour cream to the batter for every two people you are feeding. This makes an incredibly rich pancake and doubles as an excellent waffle batter when made thick.

PUMPKIN PANCAKES

These are surprisingly good. They taste like pumpkin pie. Kids love them!

AT HOME

This can be made lightweight for travel by drying the pre-spiced canned pumpkin into a fruit-leather consistency with a food dehydrator or by baking on parchment paper overnight in an oven set on 200 degrees Fahrenheit. If you are not making the pumpkin into fruit leather, you will have to freeze the appropriate amount of canned pumpkin in a plastic bag prior to your trip and store it in your soft-sided cooler for travel … unless you can find a small can of pumpkin.

IN CAMP

Prep time: 20 minutes / one frying pan or griddle

Re-hydrate pumpkin leather in hot water left over from your morning beverages or add spices and eggs to canned pumpkin in a mixing pot. Stir in pancake flour mix and add water a little at a time until consistency is about right. Remember, always err on the side of too thick because you can always add more water; thin batter is hard to flip. Heat a griddle or frying pan on a medium flame until drops of water dance on it. Lightly coat the pan with oil and fry the cakes, turning once when edges look done. Pumpkin cakes will be colorful and very aromatic.

Shopping List:	Number of Campers			
	2	**4**	**6**	**12**
Five-Mile Pancake mix	1½ c	3 c	5 c	8 c
Water or milk	1 c	1½ c	2 c	4 c
Vegetable oil or melted butter	1 T	2 T	2½ T	4 T
Eggs, beaten	1	2	2	4
Pumpkin, canned (before drying)	1 c	1½ c	3 c	5 c
SPICES:				
Vanilla Extract, real	1 t	2 t	1 T	2 T
Pumpkin Pie Spice	1 t	2 t	1 T	2 T
Brown Sugar	2 t	1 T	1½ T	3 T
Maple Syrup	2 T	4 T	½ c	1 c

B R E A K F A S T

VARIATIONS AND COMMENTS

If you are making these at home or have access to a cooler, add a half cup of plain yogurt or sour cream to the batter for every two people you are feeding. You can also top the pancakes with a dollop of vanilla yogurt as an alternative to maple syrup, giving the feel of whipped cream atop pumpkin pie.

APPLE CORNCAKES

This is a hearty variation of pancakes with hot apple compote. They are a light cake with the pleasant sweet crunch of cornbread.

AT HOME

Coat the dried apple slices with cinnamon before packing for travel. This makes them less sticky. Package eggs for travel.

IN CAMP

Prep time: 15 to 20 minutes / one frying pan, one pot

In a bowl or zip-seal plastic bag blend the dry and wet ingredients until you have a consistent batter. Pouches of dry corn muffin mix (commonly found in the baking aisle of supermarkets) work well when added 1:1 to the Five-Mile Pancake Mix as the basis for this dry batter.

Cover dried apple slices with boiling water and let stand 20 minutes or so. Add additional water to just cover the apples and bring back to a boil, reduce flame, and simmer covered until apples break down when stirred. Add additional cinnamon, brown sugar, and a pinch of nutmeg if you like. The brown sugar brings out the homemade applesauce flavor.

Heat a frying pan on medium flame until drops of water dance on it. Lightly coat the frying pan with oil and fry the cakes, turning once when the edges barely look done. These are best if you pan bake lightly. Serve with hot apple mixture spooned over the top instead of maple syrup. Although using both is even better!

Shopping List:	Number of Campers			
	2	4	6	12
PANCAKE MIX:				
½ Five-Mile Mix & ½ Corn Muffin Mix	1½ c	3 c	5 c	8 c
Vegetable oil or melted butter	1 T	2 T	2½ T	4 T
Eggs, beaten	1	2	3	5
Dried Apple Slices for compote	½ c	1 c	1½ c	3 c
Water or Milk	Add a bit, mix, and repeat until you have achieved a desired consistency that will pour into round cakes.			
SPICES:				
Cinnamon	½ t	1 t	2 t	1 T
Nutmeg	pinch	¼ t	½ t	1 t
Brown Sugar	1 t	2 t	1 T	2 T

B R E A K F A S T

VARIATIONS AND COMMENTS

Sprinkle the stack of pancakes and apples with chopped nuts. Or for an extremely decadent version, cook down some wild raspberries and sugar for a topping. Unbelievable!

60

LEMON FEATHER CAKES

Aptly named, these will be the lightest pancakes you have ever tasted. No, the egg amounts are not a misprint. This is more of an egg dish than a pancake in the traditional sense.

AT HOME
Fresh eggs are necessary for this recipe. Pack them carefully.

IN CAMP
Prep time: 20 minutes / one frying pan or griddle, one pot

You will need to separate the egg whites into a pot or bowl and drop the yolks into a zip-seal bag or another bowl large enough to accommodate all of the batter. Once you have the eggs separated, shave off the lemon zest with a pocketknife and cut into fine bits. Next add zest to the yolks along with lemon juice, milk (recon-stituted dry or canned), flour, and vanilla extract. Blend this until you have a thick batter without lumps. While the frying pan is heating, beat the egg whites with a wire whisk or fork until they form stiff peaks; fold into the yolk mixture until just blended. Batter will be highly aerated. Do not over blend.

Heat a frying pan or griddle on medium flame until drops of water dance on it. Lightly coat the pan with oil and fry the cakes, turn-ing once when edges barely look done. These will puff up to thick light cakes that are best served with a wedge of lemon squeezed over them followed by a dusting of powdered sugar.

Shopping List:	Number of Campers			
	2	4	6	12
Flour	¾ c	1½ c	2½ c	5 c
Eggs	4	8	12	24
Milk	½ c	1 c	1½ c	3 c
Vegetable oil or melted butter	1 T	2 T	2½ T	4 T
Lemons	1	1	2	3
Lemon Zest (yellow part of peel)	1 t	2 t	1 T	2 T
Lemon Juice	2 t	1 T	1½ T	3 T
SPICES:				
Vanilla Extract, real	½ t	1 t	1½ t	1 T
Powdered Sugar	1 T	1½ T	3 T	½ c

VARIATIONS AND COMMENTS
This recipe is easy to whip together and will impress the most discerning com-pany at home. The cakes are great hot or cold, with or without syrup, without any big variations. However, if you are pulling out all the stops and making a special breakfast for someone, top them with freshly whipped cream that has been flavored with a bit of orange zest and Grand Marnier. It will be worth the effort.

BREAKFAST

61

PANCAKES WITH HOT APPLE COMPOTE

I have prepared this recipe for the last fifteen years and people always love it.

AT HOME

Coat the dried apple slices with cinnamon before packing for travel. This makes them less sticky.

IN CAMP

Prep time: 15 to 20 minutes / one frying pan, one pot

In a bowl or zip-seal plastic bag blend the dry and wet ingredients until you have a consistent batter. Cover dried apple slices with boiling water and let stand 20 minutes or so. Add additional water to just cover the apples and bring back to a boil, reduce flame, and simmer covered until apples break down when stirred. Add additional cinnamon, brown sugar, and a pinch of nutmeg if you like. The brown sugar brings out the homemade applesauce flavor.

Heat a frying pan or griddle on medium flame until drops of water dance on it. Lightly coat the pan with oil and fry the cakes, turning once when edges look done. Serve with hot apple mixture spooned over the top instead of maple syrup. Using both is even better!

Shopping List:	Number of Campers			
	2	4	6	12
Five-Mile Pancake Mix	1½ c	3 c	5 c	8 c
Vegetable oil or melted butter	1 T	2 T	2½ T	4 T
Eggs	1	2	3	5
Dried Apple Slices	½ c	1 c	1½ c	3 c
Water or Milk	Add a bit, mix, and repeat until you have achieved a desired consistency that will pour into round cakes.			
SPICES:				
Cinnamon	½ t	1 t	2 t	1 T
Nutmeg	pinch	¼ t	½ t	1 t
Brown Sugar	1 t	2 t	1 T	2 T

VARIATIONS AND COMMENTS

For added flavor sprinkle your stack of pancakes and apples with chopped walnuts. By using dried apples and powdered eggs, you can make this a meal light enough to carry in your backpack.

B
R
E
A
K
F
A
S
T

Chapter 10

LUNCH & APPETIZERS

USUALLY LUNCH FALLS into the "moveable feast" category, i.e., it is often enjoyed along the journey while the kitchen is still packed away. That's when we reach for the "grab bag" of gnoshes. Whether backpacking or lightweight canoe tripping, choose the lightest items from the choices that follow. Kayak touring is nearly the same as car camping in terms of weight restrictions … okay, maybe you have to leave the cup holder bedecked lounger camp chair behind—but with a little creativity, you can live it up.

If time permits and you set up camp at lunchtime you may want to fire up the stove to serve grilled sandwiches or prepare a hot main course. Sometimes I will flip the menu around to serve a hot main meal midday and a lighter meal in the evening. This works especially well if you are traveling in bear country and would prefer not to do a lot of cooking near where you sleep.

Portable Picnics

Carbohydrates
- Grainy crackers with strong constitutions that travel well: rye crisp, Melba toast, Triscuits, bagel chips, and water crackers
- Breads that travel well include bagels, cocktail rye, whole-grain sourdoughs, English muffins, pita bread, and tortillas of all sorts

- Pastas, grains, and legumes in salads and spreads that you can make immediately after breakfast. These carry well and avoid spoilage when dressed with oil and acids like vinegar or citrus juice. Choices include: couscous, tabouli, millet, quinoa, pasta, and hummus

Proteins and Fats

- Meat and fish—like tuna, salmon, chicken, and turkey—that can be found in vacuum-sealed pouches are easy to carry and come in a wide variety of choices, including smoked and lemon pepper. Canned tuna, sardines, and smoked oysters add variety. Dry cured sausages that come vacuum-sealed, like salami, pepperoni, or Parma ham can happily make their way to the picnic.
- Hard cheeses, like cheddar and Swiss, keep well and are versatile. Wax-coated varieties keep a long time.
- Cream cheese makes great spreads and can be a tasty base for sauces. If you purchase it in a plastic tub it keeps for up to a week if unopened until needed.
- Nuts and spreads. Peanut butter is a widely available crowd pleaser, and the market also offers other terrific nut butters, including almond, cashew, and soy. Need a quick dessert? Spread peanut butter between two chocolate chip cookies—or Nutella® between two butter cookies. Almonds, cashews, peanuts, walnuts, and pecans can be eaten as is or mixed with dried fruit and M&M's to make a healthy and tasty trail mix.

Caution: Take great care to avoid taking any peanut products on a trip with someone who has a peanut allergy. Anaphylaxis can ruin your whole day.

Fruits and Veggies

Apples, carrots, plums, citrus, and even grapes carry easily to add freshness to lunches. Dried fruits and dry veggie snack mixes are great when you need to shed weight from your load. Keep in mind, though, you need to drink a lot of water when you eat dry fruits and vegetables.

Desserts

- Cookies: Gingersnaps are virtually indestructible; actually there are many commercial cookies available that travel well and taste good. Generally, the smaller and tighter the package, the better it will travel.

- Chocolate: Dark varieties are less prone to melt and with a little peanut butter spread atop they are sublime.

Hot Foods Without Cooking

When traveling in cold damp weather, there is nothing like a hot drink or cup of soup to take the chill off. You can easily provide this without unearthing the stove simply by carrying a variety of teas and dry soup mixes that only require hot water. The key is to fill up a thermos or two with boiling water in the morning as you are breaking camp and keep it available with the lunch grab bag for the midday meal.

Appetizers

My Kiwi friend Ian always says, "Michael, let's have something to eat while we're thinking about what we're going to have to eat!" Ian has the metabolism of a hummingbird.

SPICY AND SPEEDY CHEESE DIP

No cooking needed for this fast and easy crowd pleaser that works equally well served with crackers or tortilla chips.

IN CAMP
Prep time: 2 minutes / one bowl, no cooking required

Run a knife around the inside edge of the cream cheese and try to upend the tub into a waiting bowl to retain its shape. Open a small tin of salsa and simply pour it on top of the cream cheese for dipping.

Shopping List:	Number of Campers			
	2	4	6	12
Soft Cream Cheese, 8 oz. tub	1	1	2	3
Crackers or Tortilla Chips	8 oz	12 oz	18 oz	32 oz
Salsa, small tin	1	1	1	2

HERBS AND SPICES:
Sprinkle with chopped fresh cilantro for style points.

VARIATIONS AND COMMENTS:
Try different kinds of salsa: green, ranchero, or chipotle (quite hot). The cream cheese takes the sting out of the heat. For something a bit different and less spicy, pour pepper jelly over the cream cheese for a terrific hot and sweet variation.

L

U

N

C

H

HUMMUS WITH PITA AND VEGGIES

This fast and easy crowd pleaser works equally well with rice crackers, cut-up veggies, or wedges of toasted pita if you happen to have a stove out. Dry hummus is usually pretty bland, but with this cast of supporting characters, it is a great alternative to the usual suspects that show up at lunch.

AT HOME
Find instant hummus mix in the international section of your supermarket or the bulk section of a food co-op. Package the instant hummus mix into a zip-seal plastic bag.

IN CAMP
Prep time: 15 minutes / one bowl, no cooking required

Blend the dry hummus mix with lemon juice, olive oil, fresh garlic, and a little drinking water at a time. While you are cutting up veggies or toasting the pita bread let the hummus rest about ten minutes for the flavors to meld. You might need to add a bit more water and give it another stir just before you serve.

Shopping List:	Number of Campers			
	2	**4**	**6**	**12**
Dry Hummus Mix	1 c	2 c	3 c	4 c
Lemons for juice (can use Balsamic Vinegar)	1	1	2	3
Olive Oil	2 t	1 T	1+ T	2 T
Garlic Cloves, minced	1	2	3	5
Pita Bread, Crackers, etc	8 oz	12 oz	18 oz	32 oz
Veggies (options below) total weight	8 oz	12 oz	18 oz	32 oz
Carrots, sticks or baby				
Zucchini, sticks				
Turnip, sliced				
Sweet Pepper slices				

HERBS AND SPICES:
A little cayenne pepper in the hummus adds a great zip.

VARIATIONS AND COMMENTS
Try adding bruschetta mix or a small tin of chopped black olives into the hummus for a nice twist. Or serve with Greek olives as they don't need refrigeration and travel well.

L
U
N
C
H

EASY QUESADILLAS

This is one of the most popular appetizers on our trips and it is extremely easy and quick to make.

AT HOME

Put all the fixin's for this snack in a stuff sack so you are able to whip it together quickly. You can turn this into a lighter version for backpacking by drying the salsa into leather and reconstituting it on the trail. I favor the very small tins of salsa found in the Mexican section of the grocery store.

IN CAMP

Prep time: 5 to 10 minutes / one pan

Spread softened cream cheese in a thin layer on one side of a fajita-sized flour tortilla and drop into a dry frying pan on medium-high heat. Sprinkle a little salsa on top and put another flour tortilla on top. Flip when you smell the bottom tortilla burning a bit. Give it a couple of minutes until the bottom starts smelling a bit singed, remove to a plate, and start another. Quarter with a sharp knife and serve wedges after they cool slightly.

Shopping List:	Number of Campers			
	2	4	6	12
Flour Tortillas (fajita size)	2	4	6	12
Cream Cheese, soft	2 oz	4 oz	6oz	12 oz
Salsa	2 oz	3 oz	4 oz	6 oz

HERBS AND SPICES:

Chili Powder, to taste

VARIATIONS AND COMMENTS

People will continue to eat these as long as you are willing to make them. Add black beans, sautéed onions, and bell peppers to turn this into a main course. You can add virtually anything to this with good results, but I like the simplicity of this recipe and the utter speed involved in getting a great tasting snack into hungry mouths. Kids love this, too.

L

U

N

C

H

BAKED BRIE OR CAMEMBERT

An elegant appetizer that is easy to make and impressive enough to earn you big points with your fellow travelers. Best served with a tin cup of white wine.

AT HOME
Package herb-flavored breadcrumbs in a zip-seal bag.

IN CAMP

Prep time: 20 minutes / one covered pan, frybake pan, or Woody

Preheat covered pot, outback oven, or other baking device on low heat. Using a heat-diffuser plate aids in heating your pan more evenly. Beat one egg in a bowl and roll the unwrapped whole cheese (must be whole cheese with rind) in the egg, then evenly coat with herbed breadcrumbs by dropping coated cheese in the zip-seal bag. Place the wheel of cheese in the bottom of the heated pot, cover, and gently bake for 10 minutes. Serve in the middle of a plate surrounded by crackers or crusty sliced French bread. Brie will swell a bit and be a molten mass that spreads easily with a knife. Even folks who normally don't like this type of cheese will love this.

Shopping List:	Number of Campers			
	2	4	6	12
Whole Tinned or Boxed Cheese	1	1	1	2
Crackers or French Bread	4 oz	8 oz	12 oz	24 oz
Egg	1	1	1	2
Herbed Breadcrumbs	1 oz	1 oz	1 oz	2 oz

HERBS AND SPICES:
Sprinkle coarsely ground black pepper on the cheese before baking.

VARIATIONS AND COMMENTS
Try various breads and crackers for this. It is good on just about everything.

L
U
N
C
H

SPEEDY NACHOS

This works great as a quick snack for a group or as a main course for a few people.

AT HOME

Package instant bean mix and the dried onion and other spices in a zip-seal bag.

IN CAMP

Prep time: 15 minutes / one covered frying pan

Heat enough water in a covered pan to rehydrate bean and spice mixture. Pour the dry bean mix into a bowl and stir in hot water. Let it soak for a bit. Stir again. Put frying pan on low heat to preheat. Using a heat-diffuser plate helps heat your pan more evenly. Put a layer of tortilla chips on the bottom of the heating pan, dollop bits of the bean mixture onto the chips and sprinkle shredded cheddar cheese on the beans. Repeat the process with a second layer, cover, and let heat through for 8 to10 minutes or until cheese is thoroughly melted. Enjoy.

Shopping List:	Number of Campers			
	2	4	6	12
Tortilla Chips (12 oz. bag)	1	1	1	2
Instant Refried Beans	2 oz	3 oz	4 oz	8 oz
Dried Onion Flakes	1 T	1½ T	2 T	3 T
Cheddar Cheese, shredded	½ c	1 c	1½ c	3 c

HERBS AND SPICES:
Add to dry bean mixture before adding hot water:

Garlic Powder	½ t	¾ t	1 t	1½ t
Ground Cumin	½ t	¾ t	1 t	1½ t
Chili Powder	½ t	¾ t	1 t	1½ t
Black Pepper, to taste				
Cayenne Pepper, to taste				

L

U

N

VARIATIONS AND COMMENTS

C

You can make salsa from dried mixes or reconstitute some salsa leather you've made with a food dehydrator. The bean mixture also makes a terrific dip for crackers or tortilla chips if you stir in the cheese while it is hot.

H

Chapter 11

THE MAIN COURSE

The following recipes were created over the last twenty-five years while guiding in the backcountry. They are organized by type, starting with side dishes and salads and graduating from easy to impressive (and still easy) entrees.

GARLIC SMASHED SPUDS

Comfort food as good as a warm hug from your mom.

AT HOME

Backpack version: mix potato flakes with a good quality dry chicken soup base, garlic powder, milk powder, and Butter Buds to get a tasty side dish that only requires boiling water. If weight isn't a big concern, then find some nice red or gold potatoes and clean them at home. Pack them whole in a mesh sack for travel.

IN CAMP

Prep time: 20 minutes / one pot

Backpack version: Bring appropriate amount of water to a boil, add dry ingredients, lower heat, and simmer for 5 minutes. Season to taste with salt and pepper.

Fresh spuds: Pour a small amount of olive oil in a pot; put on low heat. Add minced fresh garlic and sauté gently until garlic begins to brown. Add chopped potatoes (skins and all) and water. Cover. Bring to a boil and steam for 10 minutes until potatoes soften. Turn off the flame, drain some of the water, add cream cheese, and mash with a fork or the bottom of a clean water bottle.

Shopping List:	Number of Campers			
	2	4	6	12
BACKPACK VERSION:				
Potato Flakes	1 c	2 c	3 c	6 c
Soup Base or Broth Mix	1 T	2 T	3 T	½ c
Dried Milk (full cream)	1 T	2 T	3 T	½ c
HERBS AND SPICES:				
Garlic Powder	1 t	2 t	1 T	2 T
Butter Buds	1 t	2 t	1 T	2 T
Black Pepper, to taste				
FRESH SPUDS VERSION:				
Red Potatoes, chopped	1 lb	2 lbs	3 lbs	6 lbs
Garlic Cloves, minced	4	6	8	16
Cream Cheese (Neufchatel works)	4 oz	4 oz	8 oz	16 oz
Butter Buds	1 t	2 t	1 T	2 T
Dried Milk (full cream)	1 T	2 T	3 T	½ c

VARIATIONS AND COMMENTS

My favorite is to sauté chopped onion with the garlic before adding the potato chunks. This is good as a base for stir-fries as well as a great comfort combo with chicken or turkey and gravy. This recipe once blossomed into a full-on Thanksgiving dinner within sight of three glaciers in Alaska. Watch for amounts of MSG (monosodium glutamate) in soup bases. It doesn't get along well with some people's systems.

DUMPLINGS FOR CHILI AND STEWS

Anything freshly baked in the backcountry will raise your status from cook to guru. Your deity status is virtually ensured by the steam rolling from under the cover of your simmering pot when you turn out these dumplings.

AT HOME
Package all of the dry ingredients in a zip-seal plastic bag.

IN CAMP
Pour a small amount of water into the dry mix in the zip-seal bag; close and fondle till blended. Add water a little at a time until you get a sticky dough consistency, not pancake batter. Be sure you have at least an inch and a half of headroom between dinner and the lid so you won't blow the top. Spoon out dough onto bubbling chili or stew, cover, and sneak a look after ten minutes. A pine needle ought to come out of the dough clean when they are done. These dumplings are tasty even when they are a bit underdone. Basically it is Dutch oven cooking on your backpacking stove.

Shopping List:	Number of Campers			
	2	4	6	12
FOR REGULAR DUMPLINGS:				
Bisquick or equivalent mix	1 c	2 c	3 c	5 c
FOR CORNBREAD DUMPLINGS:				
Martha White or other just-add-water mixes	1 c	2 c	3 c	5 c

VARIATIONS AND COMMENTS
For a tasty twist to regular dumplings add some dried basil, onion, and parmesan cheese. Try adding red pepper flakes and some shredded cheddar cheese to the cornbread dough for an outstanding chili feast. The key to these recipes is to watch your heat and amounts of water carefully. Once the dough goes in, no more stirring; so make sure the stove is on low simmer before you cover the pan and walk away for a bit. I once made the dumplings with beer; the kids hated them. The rest of us thought they were right fine though.

GONZO RICE

This is a great side dish for south-of-the-border favorites or can act as a main dish with the addition of some black beans and/or canned chicken.

AT HOME

Mix all ingredients in a zip-seal plastic bag.

IN CAMP
Prep time: 25 minutes / one pot

Pour dry ingredients into a pot. Add appropriate amount of water and soup base; bring to a boil. Reduce heat, cover, and simmer for 20 minutes. Fluff with a fork and serve with salsa.

Shopping List:	Number of Campers			
	2	4	6	12
White Basmati rice	½ c	1 c	1½ c	3 c
Onion Flakes, dried	1 oz	1½ oz	2 oz	3 oz
Dried Bell Peppers	1 oz	1½ oz	2 oz	3 oz
Freeze-dried Yellow Corn	1 oz	2 oz	3 oz	6 oz
Chopped Sun-dried Tomatoes	1 oz	2 oz	3 oz	6 oz
Chicken or Vegetable Soup Base	1 oz	1.5 oz	2 oz	3 oz
HERBS AND SPICES:				
Chili Powder	½ t	1 t	1½ t	3 t
Dried Parsley	Pinch	½ t	1 t	2 t
Hot Red Pepper Flakes, to taste				
Black Pepper, to taste				

S I D E

D I S H E S

VARIATIONS AND COMMENTS

Any white rice is fine, I just like the way Basmati cooks. Brown rice works well but use a parboiled variety to cut down on the cooking time. You can also do the same treatment to couscous as a base for a twist. For a main dish, simply add dried cooked black beans.

CINNAMON PLANTAINS

This is a great side dish to serve with fish or beans and rice combinations to create a meal with a Caribbean appeal.

AT HOME

Choose ripe plantains that are yellow and have black spots. They may be labeled as platano if you have Latino markets near you. As they ripen they will become yellow and black—blacker than overripe bananas. Even in this state they are still hardy travelers. Related to bananas, culturally, they are used more like potatoes.

IN CAMP
Prep time: 15 minutes / one pan

Heat butter in a frying pan on low heat. Split plantain peels with a knife, peel them off, and slice the plantains on an angle into long slices about a quarter inch thick. Brown them on one side in the butter. Sprinkle with cinnamon while browning, turn and repeat. Just before they are completely browned on the flip side, add a little rum or brandy to caramelize the sugars. Cook off the alcohol and remove from pan. Caution, they may flame up but this is part of kitchen theatre. Sprinkle with sugar and lime juice just after the rum to serve as a dessert.

Shopping List:	Number of Campers			
	2	4	6	12
Plantains	1	3	4	8
Butter	1 T	2 T	3 T	½ c
Rum or Brandy	1 T	2 T	3 T	2/3 c

SPICES:
Cinnamon, to taste

VARIATIONS AND COMMENTS

Plantains look like bananas and are starchy. They travel well and can be prepared in a number of ways. You can substitute medium-ripe bananas, but they taste much sweeter and don't travel as well. If you use plantains as a dessert you come out with Bananas Foster as a kayaking dessert. How bad can that be?

SIDE DISHES

CRUNCHY CABBAGE & APPLE SALAD

Moving well beyond the idea that salad is lettuce with garnishes.

AT HOME

Package fresh veggies together in a breathable bag. Store dressing in an appropriately sized leak-proof plastic bottle.

IN CAMP

Prep time: 10 minutes / one pot

Combine everything about 15 minutes before you want to eat. Hey, why suffer when salads are so easy and provide a second course with no cooking?

Shopping List:	Number of Campers			
	2	4	6	12
Sweet Onion, chopped	¼ c	½ c	1 c	1½ c
Red Bell Pepper, diced	½	1	2	3
Cabbage, shredded (Chinese, red, or white)	2 c	4 c	6 c	10 c
Dried Cherries	1 T	2 T	¼ c	½ c
Apple, chopped	1	1½	2	3
Dressing: any sort of oil based	3oz	6oz	8oz	12oz

HERBS AND SPICES:
Black Pepper, to taste

VARIATIONS AND COMMENTS

Dress up this salad with creamy horseradish sauce and a splash of lime juice instead of commercial dressing. Cabbage has an undeserved bad reputation. It is versatile, comes in lots of textures and colors, and is virtually immortal.

S

A

L

A

D

S

 76

PSEUDO-CAESAR SALAD

This is a delightfully crunchy salad that pairs well with pastas, fish and a nice pinot gris.

AT HOME
Package fresh veggies together in a breathable bag. Store dressing in an appropriately sized leak-proof plastic bottle—a wide-mouthed Nalgene® is ideal.

IN CAMP
Prep time: 10 minutes / one pot

Combine everything about 15 minutes before you want to eat.

Shopping List:	Number of Campers			
	2	**4**	**6**	**12**
Sweet Onion, chopped	¼ c	½ c	1 c	1½ c
Red Bell Pepper, diced	½	1	2	3
Cabbage, shredded (Chinese, Napa or celery)	2 c	4 c	6 c	10 c
Dried Cherries	1 T	2 T	¼ c	½ c
Walnuts, chopped	1 T	2 T	¼ c	½ c
Dressing	2 oz	3 oz	4 oz	8 oz
Croutons	Enough to sprinkle liberally			

HERBS AND SPICES:
Dress with Newman's Own Caesar salad dressing. It is tough to beat for an easy way out.

VARIATIONS AND COMMENTS
Most of these ingredients will keep for nearly a week without refrigeration; so you can enjoy crisp salad near the end of a trip. Napa cabbage has a tender texture and shape more akin to Romaine lettuce.

S
A
L
A
D
S

SANTA FE SALAD

As a lunch, side dish, or a relish, this salad has plenty of hearty zip.

AT HOME

Package fresh veggies together in a breathable bag. If you are using fresh cilantro, see page 39 for tips on how to pack fresh herbs for travel.

IN CAMP

Prep time: 5 minutes / one pot

Chop onions and peppers; combine with all other ingredients a few minutes before you want to eat. Dress with lime juice and sprinkle liberally with black pepper and chili powder.

Shopping List:	Number of Campers			
	2	4	6	12
Sweet Onion, chopped	¼ c	½ c	1 c	1½ c
Red Bell Pepper, diced	½	1	2	3
Yellow Corn, canned, drained	4-6 oz	12 oz	15 oz	30 oz
Black Beans, canned, drained & rinsed	4-6 oz	12 oz	15 oz	30 oz
Garlic Cloves, minced	1	2	3	5
Limes, for juice	1	2	3	4
Olive Oil	1 T	1½ T	2 T	3 T
Balsamic Vinegar	1 T	1½ T	2 T	3 T
HERBS AND SPICES:				
Chili Powder	1 t	1½ t	2 t	1 T
Cumin	1 t	1½ t	2 t	1 T
Cilantro, freshly chopped, to taste				
Black Pepper to taste				
Red Pepper Sauce to taste				

S
A
L
A
D
S

VARIATIONS AND COMMENTS

Add balsamic vinegar and olive oil with the lime juice. Skip the chili powder and add fresh mint with the cilantro for a completely different and fresh taste. A little red pepper sauce will give it just the right kick.

CURRIED SLAW

For those who enjoy curry, this side salad is addictive and I promise you will want to make this at home.

AT HOME
Package fresh veggies together in a breathable bag. You can find small containers of mayonnaise or horseradish sauce in supermarkets or small packets from fast food restaurants.

IN CAMP
Prep time: 10 minutes / one pot

Combine everything about 15 minutes before you want to eat.

Shopping List:	Number of Campers			
	2	**4**	**6**	**12**
Cabbage, shredded (Chinese, red, or white)	2 c	4 c	6 c	10 c
Raisins	1 T	2 T	¼ c	½ c
Apple, chopped	1	1½	2	3
Dressing: Mayo or Horseradish Sauce	3 oz	6 oz	8 oz	12 oz
HERBS AND SPICES:				
Curry Powder	1 t	2 t	1 T	1.5T
Black Pepper, to taste				

VARIATIONS AND COMMENTS
Dress up this salad with creamy horseradish sauce and a splash of lime juice or cider vinegar.

S
A
L
A
D
S

CORN CUCUMBER SALAD

Okay, I have to admit it. We had nothing left, just a few odds and ends, near the end of a trip and we created this salad. After a few surprised looks, it was deemed a keeper.

AT HOME
Package fresh veggies together in a breathable bag.

IN CAMP
Prep time: 5 minutes / one pot

Peel and quarter cucumber lengthwise. Scrape out seeds with a spoon and slice into bite-sized pieces. Combine with other ingredients a few minutes before you want to eat. Dress with splashes of lime juice, balsamic vinegar, and olive oil. Serve. This is also great stuffed in Pita bread with cheese for lunch.

Shopping List:	Number of Campers			
	2	**4**	**6**	**12**
Cucumber (whole)	sm.	med	2	3
Red Bell Pepper, diced	½	1	2	3
Yellow Corn (canned), drained	4-6 oz	12 oz	15 oz	30 oz
Garlic Cloves, minced	1	2	3	4
Limes	1	2	3	4
Balsamic Vinegar	1 oz	2 oz	3 oz	4 oz
Olive Oil	1 oz	2 oz	3 oz	4 oz

HERBS AND SPICES:
Black Pepper, to taste
Chili Powder, to taste

VARIATIONS AND COMMENTS
Skip the chili powder and add thinly sliced red onion, olives, a bit of oregano, and feta cheese for a Greek flavor.

S
A
L
A
D
S

GREEK PASTA SALAD

This salad is simple to make and will surprise you with its explosive flavor.

AT HOME

For short trips you could prepare the salad at home or shorten the prep time by chopping the celery and carrots and storing in a zip-seal bag.

IN CAMP

Prep time: 25 minutes / one pot and a zip-seal plastic bag

Bring an appropriate amount of water to a boil. Add penne pasta. Cook until almost tender, drain, and add dressing immediately. Stir well to coat the pasta with the dressing. Add olives, feta cheese, and vegetables; mix well. Let stand in the pot to cool a bit and then transfer to a zip-seal bag or container for travel.

Shopping List:	Number of Campers			
	2	4	6	12
Penne or similar pasta	8 oz	16 oz	24 oz	3 lbs
Sun-dried Tomatoes, chopped	1 oz	2 oz	3 oz	6 oz
Celery, chopped	½ c	1 c	1½ c	3 c
Carrots, chopped	½ c	1 c	1½ c	3 c
Red Bell Pepper, diced	½ c	1 c	1½ c	3 c
Feta cheese (crumbled w/basil and tomato)	2 oz	4 oz	6 oz	12 oz
Olives, sliced (black or pitted Greek)	2 oz	4 oz	6 oz	12 oz
Greek Salad Dressing (your choice)	½ c	1 c	1½ c	3 c

HERBS AND SPICES:
Black Pepper, to taste

VARIATIONS AND COMMENTS

This salad is best when made the day before serving. (The trick is not to eat it all beforehand.) It is a wonderful component for a paddling picnic with fresh fruit, like grapes or apples. It keeps well in moderate temperatures. Any crumbled feta cheese will work fine, but the type with basil and sun-dried tomato does very nicely.

S
A
L
A
D
S

JICAMA CARROT SALAD

When so much backcountry food has a soft texture, it is refreshing to add some serious fresh crunch to your diet.

AT HOME
Package fresh veggies together in a breathable bag. Bring fresh limes for an extra-fresh kick.

IN CAMP
Prep time: 10 minutes / one pot

Peel and slice jicama, grate carrot; combine with lime juice and spices fifteen minutes before serving to let the flavors mingle.

Shopping List:	Number of Campers			
	2	**4**	**6**	**12**
Jicama	½	1	2	3
Carrots	2	4	6	10
Apple, chopped (optional)	1	1½	2	3
Lime Juice, fresh	1 T	2 T	3 T	4 T

HERBS AND SPICES:
Black Pepper, to taste
Chili Powder, several dashes

VARIATIONS AND COMMENTS
Yeah, I know it sounds weird, but this salad is good. For other twists, add canned pineapple, canned mandarin oranges, or a little chopped onion. Yes, even with the chili powder. Chilies and pineapples are a hot combo in Baja.

S
A
L
A
D
S

Out of Gas

*"I am going to stick my head in that pot and eat my way out!"
Danny said, eyeing the huge cauldron of mac 'n cheese. That was
one of his least colorful remarks. Danny was 16 years old and
developing his expertise at expletives. A promising amateur, he
definitely could turn pro.*

*But right then, Danny was simply hungry. He and fourteen other
ravenous teenagers had paddled 87 miles in thirteen hours on a
handful of rice and instant chocolate pudding. Another guide and
I were shepherding them along two hundred miles of Yukon River
by canoe, and the company we were working for under-budgeted
for both food and time.*

*Sharing twenty boxes of mac 'n cheese and a dozen loaves of
white bread turned out to be a bonding experience after a hard
day of earnest paddling—but I don't recommend it.*

*When planning meals for a trip longer than a weekend, bring
a small cushion of extra supplies in case you get stuck due to
weather or any host of other unforeseen delays. Extra oatmeal,
rice, dried potatoes, or couscous are lightweight and versatile
emergency items. Also, be sure you know how much your traveling
companions eat. If you are paddling with a weightlifter who
consumes 6,000 calories a day, you need to pack accordingly.*

Food is fuel—don't run out of gas.

Rudy's Island Pancakes (see p. 57)

GREEK CABBAGE SALAD

Most of these items will keep for nearly a week without refrigeration so you can enjoy crisp salad toward the end of a trip.

AT HOME
Package fresh veggies together in a breathable bag. Store dressing in an appropriately sized leak-proof plastic bottle.

IN CAMP
Prep time: 10 minutes / one pot

Combine everything about 15 minutes before you want to eat.

Shopping List:	Number of Campers			
	2	4	6	12
Sweet Onion, chopped	¼ c	½ c	1 c	1½ c
Red Bell Pepper, diced	½	1	2	3
Chinese or Celery Cabbage, shredded	2 c	4 c	6 c	10 c
Greek Olives	6	12	18	30+
Feta Cheese, crumbled	1 oz	2 oz	3 oz	6 oz

HERBS AND SPICES:
You can make your own dressing by mixing olive oil, fresh minced garlic, wine vinegar, basil, salt, and pepper. Or you can purchase Greek-style dressing at the store.

VARIATIONS AND COMMENTS
This salad is also good with Caesar dressing.

S
A
L
A
D
S

ANGEL HAIR PASTA WITH SHRIMP
IN CAJUN-CREAM SAUCE

This is really a rich tasting meal and is great when you're short on time because it is so quick to prepare.

AT HOME

Peel shrimp and put in a zip-seal plastic bag. Add the juice of two limes. Freeze.

IN CAMP

Prep time: 20 minutes / two pots

In a large pot, bring water to a boil for the angel hair pasta. In a second pot, sauté fresh garlic in olive oil for two minutes on medium heat. Add thawed shrimp and sauté for 5 minutes in the garlic infused oil. Remove shrimp. Add all of the chopped vegetables to the garlic mixture; sauté for 5 to 7 minutes until onion is tender and clear. Add tomato sauce, spices, and evaporated milk. Cook gently for 10 minutes. While sauce is simmering, add pasta to the hot water and boil until almost tender (two minutes). When the pasta goes in the water is a good time to return the shrimp to the sauce for a final heat-through. Drain pasta, combine, and enjoy.

Shopping List:	Number of Campers			
	2	**4**	**6**	**12**
Angel Hair Pasta	8 oz	16 oz	24 oz	3 lbs
Tomato Sauce, canned	4 oz	8 oz	8 oz	16 oz
Onion, chopped	4 oz	8 oz	12 oz	24 oz
Red Bell Pepper, chopped	½	1	1	2
Evaporated Milk	4 oz	4 oz	8 oz	16 oz
Shrimp	½ lb	1 lb	1 lb	2 lbs
HERBS AND SPICES:				
Cajun Spice	½ t	1 t	1½ t	2 t
Worcestershire Sauce	½ t	1 t	1½ t	2 t
Garlic Cloves, minced	3	4	6	10
Tabasco, to taste				
Black Pepper, to taste				

P
A
S
T
A

VARIATIONS AND COMMENTS

For a zestier sauce, add fresh chopped cilantro, a bit of lime juice, and an extra squirt of red pepper sauce. The ingredients for this recipe can be made lighter weight for travel by using dried veggies, dry instant milk, concentrated tomato paste in a tube and omitting the shrimp. If you do this, remember to add salt to the sauce to counteract the sweetness of the concentrated paste.

PESTO ANGEL HAIR PASTA WITH SUN-DRIED TOMATOES

Easy, quick, and tasty makes this recipe a winner for any trip.

AT HOME
Package all of the dried ingredients together (except the pasta).

IN CAMP
Prep time: 15 minutes / two pots

In a large pot, bring water to a boil for the angel hair pasta. In a second pot, sauté the fresh garlic and dried veggies in olive oil. Mix dry pesto packet according to directions and add to veggies and garlic. Simmer. When heated through remove from heat. When pasta is done, drain. Pour sauce on pasta, mix well, and serve.

Shopping List:	Number of Campers			
	2	4	6	12
Angel Hair Pasta	6 oz	12 oz	18 oz	36 oz
Sun-dried Tomatoes, chopped	½ oz	1 oz	1½ oz	2 oz
Dried Onion, flakes	1 t	2 t	1 T	2 T
Dried Bell Pepper	1 t	2 t	1 T	2 T
Garlic Cloves, minced	3	4	6	10
Instant Pesto	½	1	1½	3

HERBS AND SPICES:
Black Pepper, to taste
Parmesan Cheese, grated, to taste

VARIATIONS AND COMMENTS
You'll find packets of dried pesto mix in the spice isle of your supermarket or at your local food co-op. If you prefer to use bottled or frozen pesto, do so. For a fuller flavor, use white wine instead of water to hydrate the sauce. Other vegetables like fresh broccoli or freeze-dried peas are good additions. Pine nuts and chopped pecans or walnuts add a wonderful crunch when sprinkled on top.

P
A
S
T
A

SANTA FE RIGATONI

Colorful vegetarian fare that will make you forget you are far from a refrigerator.

AT HOME
If you are using freeze-dried corn and dried cooked black beans, package together with the spices and dried tomatoes.

IN CAMP
Prep time: 25 minutes / two pots

In a large pot, bring water to a boil for the rigatoni. In a second pot, sauté the fresh garlic in olive oil on medium heat for two minutes. Add canned corn (do not drain), chopped sun-dried tomatoes, onions, peppers, black beans with 20 percent more water than called for, and the spices. Cover pan and simmer for 15 minutes. Five minutes into the simmering process, start boiling the pasta. Drain pasta when done. Combine with sauce. Serve and enjoy.

Shopping List:	Number of Campers			
	2	**4**	**6**	**12**
Rigatoni Pasta	8 oz	16 oz	24 oz	3 lbs
Sun-dried Tomatoes, chopped	1 oz	2 oz	3 oz	6 oz
Canned Corn (15 oz), with water	4 oz	8 oz	12 oz	24 oz
Instant Black Beans	2 oz	4 oz	6 oz	12 oz
Onion, dried	½ oz	1	2	3
Bell Peppers, diced	½ oz	1	2	3
HERBS AND SPICES:				
Chili Powder	½ t	1 t	1½ t	2 t
Worcestershire Sauce	½ t	1 t	1½ t	2 t
Cumin	¼ t	½ t	¾ t	1½ t
Black Pepper, to taste				

P
A
S
T
A

VARIATIONS AND COMMENTS
For a zestier sauce add chopped fresh cilantro, a bit of lime juice, and a squirt of red pepper sauce. Chicken, whether leftover at home, canned or from a pouch are all welcome additions. The ingredients for this recipe can be made lighter weight for travel by using freeze-dried corn and dried bell peppers.

BACKCOUNTRY PRIMAVERA

Rich-tasting without the heavy feeling of traditional cream sauces. This also makes a good lunch salad.

AT HOME

Prepackage the chicken or vegetable soup base. Watch for amounts of MSG (monosodium glutamate) in soup bases. It doesn't get along well with some people's systems.

IN CAMP

Prep time: 25 minutes / two pots

In a large pot, bring water to a boil for the rigatoni. In a second pot, sauté the fresh garlic in olive oil on medium heat for two minutes. Add onion and peppers; sauté for another five minutes or until onion is clear and tender. Add white wine, the soup base, basil, water, and remaining chopped vegetables. Cover pan and simmer for 5 minutes. Stir in cream cheese. Start boiling pasta while the cream cheese melts and becomes creamy. Sauce should reach proper creamy texture just as the vegetables become tender. Drain rigatoni noodles when done, add sauce and sprinkle with coarse black pepper.

Shopping List:	Number of Campers			
	2	4	6	12
Rigatoni Pasta	½ lb	1 lb	1½ lb	3 lb
Onion, chopped	½	1	2	3
Red Bell Peppers, diced	½	1	2	3
Garlic Cloves, minced	3	4	6	10
Broccoli (head)	½	1	1	2
Carrots, sliced	2	3	5	8
White Wine	½ c	1 c	1½ c	3 c
Water	½ c	1 c	1½ c	3 c
Cream Cheese	4 oz	6 oz	8 oz	12 oz
HERBS AND SPICES:				
Basil, dried	1 t	2 t	1 T	2 T
Instant Chicken or Vegetable Soup base	2 t	1 T	1½ T	2 T
Black Pepper, to taste				

P
A
S
T
A

VARIATIONS AND COMMENTS

For a crunchy treat, add roasted cashews or almonds. Use cauliflower instead of broccoli or fresh basil instead of dried. Light cream cheese (Neufchatel) works well with this recipe. Non-fat cream cheese does not.

LINGUINI WITH CREAMY CRAB SAUCE

With a splash of color from sweet red peppers, this rich meal will keep you warm on cool evenings. It is delicious and easy to prepare.

AT HOME
Pack fresh veggies in a mesh bag so they can breathe.

IN CAMP
Prep time: 25 minutes / two pots

In a large pot, bring water to a boil for the linguini. In a second pot, briefly sauté the fresh garlic, onion, and peppers in olive oil on medium heat for flavors to mingle. Add crab, wine, and cream cheese. Heat to a boil; reduce heat and simmer for 10 minutes. Continue stirring until sauce is creamy. Your 10-minute simmer is a good time to start the pasta, so they finish at the same time. When pasta is done, drain. Mix with sauce. Garnish with a couple slices of fresh red peppers and fresh basil.

Shopping List:	Number of Campers			
	2	4	6	12
Linguini Noodles	8 oz	16 oz	24 oz	3 lbs
Crab Meat, (6 oz can)	1	2	3	4
Onion, diced	½	1	2	3
Red Bell Pepper, diced	½	1	1½	3
Cream Cheese	4 oz	6 oz	8 oz	12 oz
White Wine	½ c	1 c	1½ c	2 c
Garlic Cloves, minced	3	5	7	12
HERBS AND SPICES:				
Basil, dried	¼ t	½ t	1 t	2 t
Black Pepper, to taste				

VARIATIONS AND COMMENTS
Substitute fresh basil for the dried basil and add a handful of snow peas. The crunch of a few pine nuts tossed on top will be long remembered, too.

P

A

S

T

A

PASTA WITH WHITE-WINE CLAM SAUCE

This quick recipe always draws raves from my clients and is worth the weight of the canned clams.

AT HOME
Simply bag everything and label for travel.

IN CAMP
Prep time: 25 minutes / two pots

In a large pot, bring water to a boil for the rigatoni. In a second pot, sauté the fresh garlic on medium heat for two minutes. Add clams and juice, olives, white wine, seasonings, veggies, and artichoke hearts. Cover and simmer for 15 minutes.

Shopping List:	Number of Campers			
	2	4	6	12
Rigatoni Pasta	8 oz	16 oz	24 oz	3 lbs
Sun-dried Tomatoes, chopped	1 oz	2 oz	3 oz	6 oz
Clams (6 oz can)	1	2	3	4
Artichoke Hearts, canned	2 oz	4 oz	6 oz	12 oz
Black Olives, sliced (4 oz can)	½	1	1	2
Onion, chopped	½	1	2	3
White Wine	½ c	1 c	1½ c	2 c
Garlic Cloves, minced	3	5	7	12
HERBS AND SPICES:				
Basil, dried	¼ t	½ t	1 t	2 t
Worcestershire Sauce	¼ t	½ t	1 t	2 t
Balsamic Vinegar	¼ t	½ t	1 t	2 t
Black Pepper, to taste				

VARIATIONS AND COMMENTS
Use Greek olives and/or add some sliced carrot.

P
A
S
T
A

PENNE CARBONARA

Refreshingly light, yet hearty and quick to make. This is a good cool weather crowd pleaser with many good variations.

AT HOME

You can use either chicken or vegetable soup base. If using a liquid paste style base, package in a tightly sealed plastic bag. Watch for amounts of MSG (monosodium glutamate) in soup bases. It can be a headache trigger for many folks.

IN CAMP

Prep time: 20 minutes / two pots

In a large pot, bring water to a boil for the penne pasta. In a second pot, sauté the fresh garlic on medium heat for two minutes. Add chopped veggies and diced ham (or bacon); simmer for another 10 minutes. Add water and/or wine, soup mix, and cream cheese. Simmer until cream cheese melts and you have a smooth creamy texture. Continue stirring. Add pasta to water and boil just after you've added your cream cheese to melt. Drain pasta just short of when you think it is done. Stir in cream sauce and serve.

Shopping List:	Number of Campers			
	2	**4**	**6**	**12**
Penne Pasta	9 oz	20 oz	32 oz	4 lbs
Onion, diced	½	1	2	3
Sweet Red Bell Pepper, diced	½	1	2	3
Smoked Ham or Bacon, cubed	3 oz	6 oz	8 oz	1 lb
Water and/or White Wine	1 c	1½ c	2 c	3 c
Cream Cheese, light (Neufchatel)	4 oz	6 oz	8 oz	16 oz
Garlic Cloves, minced	2	3	4	10
Lime, for juice	½	2/3	1	1
HERBS AND SPICES:				
Vegetable or Chicken Soup base	1 t	2 t	1 T	2 T
Black Pepper, to taste				

P

A

S

T

A

VARIATIONS AND COMMENTS

Add broccoli to sauce when you add the water and/or wine. For a vegetarian option, use a mixture of dried mushrooms instead of meat. Add hot red pepper flakes during the sauté process for a kick.

ZITI WITH SUN-DRIED TOMATOES AND OIL-CURED OLIVES

This hearty sauce is brawling with flavor. It will elbow its way to your taste buds under adverse conditions.

AT HOME

Package the dry ingredients (chopped tomatoes, olives, onions, peppers, and basil) together in zip-seal plastic bags. Store the ziti pasta in a separate bag.

IN CAMP

Prep time: 25 minutes / two pots

To serve for dinner, add half the water the recipe calls for to the bag of dried ingredients at lunchtime to give the sauce enough time to re-hydrate. In a large pot, bring water to a boil for the ziti. In a second pot, sauté the fresh garlic on medium heat for two minutes. Add contents of sauce bag, balsamic vinegar, and red wine. Simmer for 20 minutes. Start boiling ziti 15 minutes into the simmering of the sauce. Drain pasta, mix in sauce, and enjoy.

Shopping List:	Number of Campers			
	2	4	6	12
Ziti Pasta	8 oz	16 oz	24 oz	3 lbs
Sun-dried Tomatoes, chopped	1 oz	2 oz	3 oz	6 oz
Oil-Cured Dried Olives	1 oz	2 oz	3 oz	6 oz
Onion, dried	½ oz	1 oz	2 oz	3 oz
Bell Peppers, dried	½ oz	1 oz	2 oz	3 oz
Water (add to above ingredients)	½ c	1 c	1c	2 c
Balsamic Vinegar	½ oz	1 oz	2 oz	3 oz
Red Wine (dry)	½ c	1 c	1½ c	2 c
HERBS AND SPICES:				
Basil, dry	½ t	1 t	1½ t	2½ t
Worcestershire Sauce	½ t	1 t	1½ t	2½ t
Garlic Cloves, minced	3	6	8	12
Black Pepper, to taste				

P
A
S
T
A

VARIATIONS AND COMMENTS

Since this recipe utilizes mostly dry ingredients, it makes for lightweight portability. The longer the sauce simmers, the deeper these flavors meld. For a seafood version, add fresh shrimp or mussels and steam in the sauce for five minutes of the simmering process. You can also give the sauce a good shot of red pepper sauce to bridge the seafood and olive flavors with a little zip.

PORTABELLA MUSHROOM TORTELLINI
WITH SPICY SAUSAGE

This recipe is incredibly flavorful, filling, and great in cold weather.

AT HOME

Chop tomatoes with kitchen shears and package in a Nalgene® container with olive oil and a garlic clove or two. Package remaining items together in your dinner bag, grab your spice kit and you are ready to go.

IN CAMP

Prep time: 25 minutes / one pot

In a large pot, sauté the diced veggies and sausage in olive oil on medium heat until the onions begin to soften. Spoon most of these goodies onto a plate; add enough water to the pot to accommodate the pasta. Bring to a boil. Add dry pasta, bring back to a boil, and reduce heat, cooking until tortellini centers are almost done (taste test). Turn off heat and cover. Let the pasta mixture rest for 5 minutes. Drain off the water, stir in the sautéed mixture and crumbled Gorgonzola. Prepare for applause.

Shopping List:	Number of Campers			
	2	**4**	**6**	**12**
Mushroom Tortellini, dry (6 oz bags)	1	2	3	6
Sun-dried Tomatoes soaked in olive oil	2 oz	3 oz	4 oz	8 oz
Dry Cured Sausage, sliced thin	2 oz	4 oz	6 oz	12 oz
Onion, diced	½ c	1 c	1½ c	3 c
Bell Peppers, diced	½ c	1 c	2 c	3 c
Garlic Cloves, minced	3	4	6	10
Gorgonzola Cheese	2 oz	3 oz	4 oz	8 oz
HERBS AND SPICES:				
Basil, dry	1 t	2 t	1 T	2 T
Red Pepper Flakes	1 t	2 t	1 T	2 T
Red Pepper Sauce, dash				

P
A
S
T
A

VARIATIONS AND COMMENTS

Any dry-cured, vacuum-sealed Italian sausage will do, but try Sopressata. Black olives and marinated artichoke hearts are also terrific additions. If you want a more Greek variation, substitute herbed Feta cheese for the Gorgonzola and use pitted Kalamata olives. For backpacking, simply substitute dried veggies for the fresh ones and add more water. This dish will please a dinner crowd at home, especially when accompanied with a simple salad and a red wine that has the courage to stand up to this raucous variety of flavors.

ANGEL HAIR PASTA IN SMOKED SALMON CREAM SAUCE

This is a refreshingly light, yet hearty and quick-cooking crowd pleaser.

AT HOME

Reduce all packaging and put instant chicken or veggie base in a zip-seal sandwich bag. Watch for amounts of MSG (monosodium glutamate) in the broth, it is a good thing to avoid.

IN CAMP
Prep time: 20 minutes / two pots

In a large pot, bring water to a boil for the angel hair pasta. In a second pot, sauté the fresh garlic on medium heat for two minutes. Stir in chopped veggies, simmer for 10 minutes. Add water, wine, salmon, fresh lime juice, herbs and spices, broth mix, and cream cheese. Simmer until the cheese melts and you obtain a smooth creamy texture. During the last couple minutes add pasta to boiling water. Stir pasta frequently. Remove from heat just short of when you think the pasta is done. Drain the pasta, stir in cream sauce, and serve.

Shopping List:	Number of Campers			
	2	4	6	12
Angel Hair Pasta	9 oz	20 oz	32 oz	4 lbs
Onion, chopped	½	1	2	3
Red Pepper, diced	½	1	2	3
Smoked Salmon, vacuum-sealed	3 oz	6 oz	8 oz	1 lb
Water and/or White Wine	1 c	1½ c	2 c	3 c
Cream Cheese, light (Neufchatel)	4 oz	6 oz	8 oz	16 oz
Garlic Cloves, minced	2	3	4	10
Limes, for juice	1	2	2	3
HERBS AND SPICES:				
Basil, dry	½ t	1 t	1½ t	2½ t
Worcestershire Sauce	½ t	1 t	1½ t	2½ t
Instant Soup Base (vegetable or chicken)	1 t	2 t	1 T	2 T
Black Pepper, to taste				

VARIATIONS AND COMMENTS

Add fresh broccoli to the sauce when you add the water. Add fresh cilantro to the sauce (very good with the lime), and a squirt of red pepper sauce. Any fresh seafood will work, but smoked salmon wins out.

P
A
S
T
A

95

SHRIMP DIAVOLO

This is an Italian dish for those who love spices and shrimp. Heat, garlic, and seafood … it just doesn't get any better.

AT HOME

Peel and de-vein raw shrimp. Keep whole. Put in a zip-seal bag with a little water and freeze at least 24 hours in advance.

IN CAMP

Prep time: 25 minutes / two pots

Coat the thawed shrimp with sea salt, fresh lime juice, minced garlic and chili paste. While the shrimp are marinating, bring a large pot of water to a boil for the pasta. Get your frying pan nuclear hot. Toss the shrimp into the frying pan and stir them to avoid burning. Cook for about 4 minutes.

Pour in liquor and ignite. Actually, you are cooking on gas so it will ignite on its own—remember to keep your face from hovering over the pan if you like having eyebrows. Stir for another 30 seconds and pour off shrimp into a bowl. Total cooking time is five or six minutes. The flambé treatment makes the shrimp crispy and adds great flavor—in addition to being good theatre. Next, lightly sauté minced garlic and vegetables with olive oil in the cooled frying pan on low heat. Add tomatoes once the garlic is browned. Bring this up to simmer and start cooking the pasta. Once pasta is done, drain and mix the tomato mixture into your noodles. Top this with those spicy shrimp.

Shopping List:	Number of Campers			
	2	4	6	12
Pasta (Penne works well)	8 oz	16 oz	24 oz	3 lbs
Shrimp	¾ lb	1½ lbs	2 lbs	4 lbs
Limes	1	1	1	2
Tomatoes, diced, boxed, or canned	12 oz	18 oz	24 oz	40+ oz
Red Bell Pepper, chopped	½ c	1c	2c	3c
Onion, chopped	½ c	1 c	2 c	3 c
Gin or Rum	1 oz	2 oz	2 oz	3 oz
HERBS AND SPICES:				
Garlic Cloves, minced	3	5	8	head
Sea Salt, to taste				
Garlic Chili Paste	1 t	1½ t	2 t	1 T

P

A

S

T

A

VARIATIONS AND COMMENTS

The chili paste can be found in the international section of your grocery store or in any Asian food market. It is quite hot and often comes blended with garlic. It is handy stuff. You can use canned tomatoes for this, but if you can find chopped Romas in the Tetra Pak boxes (Pomi are great) you will have less rubbish and they have superior flavor.

ROTINI WITH
WHITE WINE SEAFOOD SAUCE

This dish is quick and easy to prepare and yields a colorful and light meal. Seafood lovers will be rabid over it. You won't have to call your crew to dinner—they will smell those lovely aromas and come running.

AT HOME
Freeze peeled and de-veined raw shrimp and scallops with a little water in a zip-seal bag. Pack fresh veggies in a mesh bag so they can breathe.

IN CAMP
Prep time: 20 minutes / two pots

In a large pot, bring water to a boil for the rotini. Cook pasta. In a second pot, briefly sauté the fresh garlic, onion, and peppers on medium heat for the flavors to mingle. Add wine and sweat for five minutes. Add seafood, cover, and steam for five minutes. Add this mixture to the drained rotini, stir in fresh chopped herbs and blend in coarsely grated Parmesan cheese. Serve.

Shopping List:	Number of Campers			
	2	4	6	12
Rotini	8 oz	16 oz	24 oz	3 lbs
Shrimp, thawed	4 oz	8 oz	12 oz	24 oz
Bay Scallops	4 oz	8 oz	12 oz	24 oz
Onion, chopped	½	1	2	3
Red Bell Pepper, diced	½	1	2	3
White Wine	½ c	1 c	1½ c	2 c
Garlic Cloves, minced	3	5	7	12
Parmesan Cheese, freshly grated	2 oz	3 oz	5 oz	8 oz
HERBS AND SPICES:				
Fresh Basil, chopped	1 oz	2 oz	3 oz	5 oz
Black Pepper, to taste				

VARIATIONS AND COMMENTS
You can substitute dried basil but it does not work as well. Or instead of basil you can use a mixture of fresh parsley and cilantro. Substitute canned clams and ground red chili peppers for the shrimp and scallops if you are looking for a longer traveling alternative.

P
A
S
T
A

COUSCOUS MEDLEY

This is a great first night out dinner when time is short and hunger is on the rise. Couscous is a lightweight and quick-cooking Moroccan style pasta that is available in a variety of flavorings in most grocery stores. This is an easy meal to prepare and has nice hearty flavors to finish a good day of hiking or paddling.

AT HOME

Soak skinless and boneless chicken breast in lemon juice for at least two hours; grill, poach, or sauté until just done. Cut into bite-sized pieces and freeze in a zip-seal bag. Combine all other dry ingredients (not the couscous) in a separate zip-seal bag.

IN CAMP
Prep time: 15 minutes / one pot

Bring appropriate amount of water to a boil for the couscous (follow directions provided). Add the spice mix, chicken, and dried ingredients. Simmer for 6 to 8 minutes before adding the couscous. Once the couscous is added, stir and reduce heat and cover pan. Steam for another 5 minutes. Turn off the stove and let the covered pot stand a few minutes longer to absorb the moisture. Fluff with a fork and serve.

Shopping List:	Number of Campers			
	2	4	6	12
Couscous (box)	1	1	24 oz	3 lbs
Sun-dried Tomatoes, chopped	1 oz	2 oz	3 oz	6 oz
Dried Oil-Cured or Kalamata Olives	1 oz	2 oz	3 oz	6 oz
Onion, dried	½ oz	1 oz	2 oz	3 oz
Bell Peppers, dried	½ oz	1 oz	2 oz	3 oz

HERBS AND SPICES:
Couscous usually comes with a spice packet that follows a general theme, like roasted garlic. Before you add anything else to the water, do a taste test. I think you will find that adding the grilled chicken breast and vegetables listed above will enhance the flavor in some positive ways.

VARIATIONS AND COMMENTS
You can easily skip the chicken to make this a vegetarian version. Canned or pouched chicken also works well. This dish is also great with some sort of hard cheese grated and sprinkled on top.

P
A
S
T
A

Recipe inspired by Nancy Thornton, a former assistant whose suggestions often added flavor to meals and kayak lessons.

LEMON THYME SHRIMP FETTUCCINI

This is a tasty meal that has show-stopping appeal. It is a little involved, but well worth the effort.

AT HOME

Freeze peeled and de-veined raw shrimp in a zip-seal bag at least 24 hours in advance. You can save time by freezing the shrimp in the citrus juice; the acid will cook the shrimp a bit and thus shorten your cooking time.

IN CAMP
Prep time: 25 minutes / one pot, one pan

Marinate the thawed shrimp in freshly squeezed lemon or lime juice for 15 minutes. While they are soaking, put pasta water on high heat and bring to a boil. In a frying pan, lightly sauté minced garlic and thyme in olive oil. Drain the shrimp while retaining the juice. Coat the shrimp with a little salt. Add the shrimp, chopped onion, and peppers to the garlic-infused oil and sauté for 5 or 6 minutes. Remove the shrimp and set aside in a bowl. Add pasta to boiling water and cook until just tender. Add remaining citrus juice marinade and zest to the frying pan. Add sugar and boil to reduce; then thicken with a bit of cornstarch. Return the shrimp to the sauce to coat. Pour sauce on Fettuccini and toss.

Shopping List:	Number of Campers			
	2	4	6	12
Fettuccini	8 oz	16 oz	24 oz	3 lbs
Shrimp	¾ lb	1½ lbs	2 lbs	4 lbs
Lemon or Lime juice, fresh	½ c	¾ c	1 c	2 c
Water	½ c	¾ c	1 c	2 c
Red Bell Pepper, diced	½ c	1 c	2 c	3 c
Onion, diced	½ c	1 c	2 c	3 c
Cornstarch	enough to thicken sauce			
HERBS AND SPICES:				
Thyme, dry	1 t	1½ t	2 t	1 T
Lemon or Lime zest	1 t	1½ t	2 t	1 T
Sugar	pinch	1 t	2 t	1 T

VARIATIONS AND COMMENTS
Broccoli and carrots are nice additions. Scallops do well in place of the shrimp. However, if you make this substitution, remember to lessen the cooking time by a minute or two.

P
A
S
T
A

CHICKEN GORGONZOLA WITH
A SMOKEY-CREAM SAUCE

This is an easy and quick recipe to make. Its great flavors redefine "dining out" for anyone you serve it to. It is rich-tasting without being exceptionally heavy.

AT HOME

Rinse skinned and boneless chicken breast. Cut into bite-sized pieces. Place in a zip- seal plastic bag with a little water or chicken broth. Freeze.

IN CAMP
Prep time: 25 minutes / two pots

In a large pot, bring water to a boil for the pasta. In a dry frying pan, char chopped onions and peppers. Turn down the heat and add olive oil, minced garlic, and chicken. Sauté until chicken is tender. Add broth (or wine), cream cheese and Gorgonzola; reduce heat, simmer, and stir. While the mixture simmers in the frying pan, add pasta to boiling water in the pot and cook until tender. Drain pasta, combine with sauce, and serve.

Shopping List:	Number of Campers			
	2	4	6	12
Rigatoni or Penne Pasta	8 oz	16 oz	24 oz	3 lbs
Cream Cheese, light (Neufchatel)	4 oz	8 oz	8 oz	16 oz
Gorgonzola	2 oz	4 oz	4 oz	8 oz
Chicken Breast, raw	1 lb	1½ lbs	2 lbs	3½ lbs
Sweet Onion, chopped	1 c	1½ c	2 c	3 c
Red Bell Pepper, diced	1 c	1½ c	2 c	3 c
Chicken Broth (or White Wine)	6 oz	12 oz	16 oz	24 oz
HERBS AND SPICES:				
Garlic Cloves, minced	5	8	12	20
Black Pepper, to taste				

VARIATIONS AND COMMENTS

P
A
S
T
A

There are many great variations on this central theme. Add fresh cilantro to sauce just before serving and top with fresh tomato slices. Sauté some sliced portabella mushrooms or re-hydrated oyster mushrooms with the onions and peppers. Substitute shrimp or a light-tasting fish for the chicken in the last few minutes of simmering the sauce. Great served with chilled white wine and crusty bread. Enjoy!

Thank you to my friend Gail who test-drove the first attempt of this recipe while on Roatan Island, Honduras. She gave it a rave review.

ONE-POT FRIED RICE

An easy, tasty, and forgiving meal that makes great use of random pantry items.

AT HOME
If you are using dried vegetables for a lightweight version, package the veggies with the rice in a zip-seal bag. For a complete vegan dish, omit the eggs.

IN CAMP
Prep time: 30 minutes / one large pot

Sauté all veggies in olive oil on medium heat for two or three minutes. Add dry rice and up the flame a bit. Stir until the rice starts to brown and is well-coated with oil. Add the soy sauce and spices; stir a bit more and then add the water. Reduce heat, cover, and simmer for 15 minutes. Stir again and add the egg. Turn off the heat, cover, and let sit for 5 minutes.

Shopping List:	Number of Campers			
	2	**4**	**6**	**12**
Onion, diced	½ c	1 c	1½ c	3 c
Red or Green Bell Pepper, diced	½ c	1 c	1½ c	3 c
Carrots, peeled and chopped	½ c	1 c	1½ c	3 c
Garlic Cloves, minced	3	4	6	12
Basmati Rice	1 c	2 c	3 c	6 c
Water	2 c	4 c	6 c	12 c
Eggs, beaten	1	2	3	6
HERBS AND SPICES				
Soy or Tamari Sauce	1 T	2 T	3 T	½ c
Ginger, (fresh if possible)	1 t	2 t	1 T	2 T
Black Pepper, to taste				

VARIATIONS AND COMMENTS
If you want to serve this as a side dish, cut the amounts in half. Any veggies are good in this recipe, including canned oriental vegetables. Dried veggies work fine and lighten the load for those wishing to backpack. Just add water to the packaged dried vegetables a few hours ahead of time to pre-hydrate. Canned chicken or shrimp can also be added to give this dish a little more protein.

R
I
C
E

SHRIMP AND VEGGIE STIR-FRY

This tasty seafood dish is easy to make and makes use of durable vegetables that will give you a good crunch.

AT HOME
Freeze raw peeled and de-veined shrimp with marinade ingredients in a zip-seal bag. Pack fresh veggies in mesh bags so they can breathe.

IN CAMP
Prep time: 20 minutes / two pots

In one pot, boil water for rice. Once the water boils add rice, cover, and reduce to simmer. Ignore it for 15 minutes. While the rice is cooking, heat a little olive oil in a large pot or sauté pan and toss in the minced garlic to flavor. Add all the chopped veggies. Stir-fry for 10 or 12 minutes; season with soy sauce. Toss in the shrimp and marinade, stir-fry for 8 more minutes. Cover. Turn off heat and let stand 5 minutes. Serve with the rice.

Shopping List:	Number of Campers			
	2	**4**	**6**	**12**
Basmati Rice	½ c	1 c	1½ c	3 c
Water	1 c	2 c	3 c	6 c
Shrimp, thawed	8 oz	1 lb	1½ lbs	3 lbs
Onion, diced	½	1	2	3
Green Pepper, diced	½	1	2	3
Carrots, peeled and sliced	½ c	1 c	1½ c	3 c
Broccoli, florets	½ c	1 c	1½ c	3 c
Garlic Cloves, minced	2	4	6	12
MARINADE FOR SHRIMP:				
Limes (juice only)	1	1	2	3
Cilantro, fresh, chopped	¼ c	1/2 c	¾ c	1 c
Garlic Cloves, minced	4	6	8	16
Red Pepper Flakes	1 t	2 t	1 T	1½ T
HERBS AND SPICES:				
Soy Sauce	2 t	1 T	2 T	3 T
Cracked Black Pepper, to taste				

R

I

C

E

VARIATIONS AND COMMENTS
Instead of rice, serve the stir-fry over Garlic Smashed Spuds.

SHRIMP AND GRITS (POLENTA)

Due to so many good friends from Charleston, South Carolina, we had to include this "low country" favorite. This is my version.

AT HOME
Peel shrimp and freeze in a zip-seal plastic bag.

IN CAMP
Prep time: 30 minutes / two pots

In a large pot, bring water, dried mushrooms, condensed milk, and soup base mix to boil for grits (also known as Polenta). Stir in corn grits, reduce heat a little, and stir often. In a second pot, sauté fresh garlic and chopped vegetables in olive oil for two minutes on medium heat. Add the thawed shrimp and sauté for 5 minutes in the garlic infused oil. Remove from heat. By this time the grits will have started to thicken—time to add salt and pepper to taste. Continue stirring and once it has reached the consistency of oatmeal, stir in Parmesan cheese. Ladle a healthy serving of grits onto each plate, top with shrimp and vegetable mixture. You may need to make a batch of sweet tea to go with this.

Shopping List:	Number of Campers			
	2	**4**	**6**	**12**
Shrimp	½ lb	1 lb	1 lb	2 lbs
Corn Grits (non-instant)	½ c	1c	1½ c	3 c
Onion, chopped	4 oz	8 oz	12 oz	24 oz
Red Bell Pepper, chopped	½	1	1	2
Garlic Cloves minced	3	5	8	12
Evaporated Milk	4 oz	4 oz	8 oz	16 oz
Chicken Soup Base	1 oz	2 oz	3 oz	4 oz
Mushrooms, dried	¼ c	1/3 c	2/3 c	1+ c
Parmesan Cheese, grated	1/3 c	2/3 c	1 c	1½ c

HERBS AND SPICES:
Tabasco, to taste—use enough and your grits turn pink
Black Pepper, to taste
Salt

VARIATIONS AND COMMENTS
For a North meets South version, add sautéed asparagus to the shrimp mixture. For extra credit add crumbled bacon bits to the top!

R
I
C
E

103

BACKCOUNTRY JAMBALAYA

Whether it is pleasantly zesty or smokin' hot, this is a rib-sticker that can be adjusted to satisfy many tastes.

AT HOME
Reduce all packaging and freeze the vacuum-sealed sausage for transport in a soft-sided cooler.

IN CAMP
Prep time: 45 minutes / one pot

In a large pot, sauté onions, peppers, and garlic in olive oil on medium heat for two minutes. Add sliced sausage, Worcestershire sauce, and Cajun seasoning. Stir-fry until sausage begins to brown. Add tomato sauce, tomatoes, water, and rice. Bring to a boil and then reduce heat to simmer for 30 minutes. Stir, reduce heat further and cover. Let stand until rice has absorbed the liquid.

Shopping List:	Number of Campers			
	2	4	6	12
Basmati Rice	½ c	1 c	1½ c	3 c
Onion, diced	½ c	1 c	2 c	3 c
Red or Green Pepper, diced	½ c	1 c	2 c	3 c
Vacuum-sealed Smoked Sausage, sliced	4 oz	8 oz	1 lb	2 lbs
Tomato Sauce	4 oz	8 oz	12 oz	20 oz
Tomatoes, canned diced	8 oz	12 oz	24 oz	32 oz
Water	1 c	1½ c	2 c	3 c
Garlic Cloves, minced	3	4	6	12
HERBS AND SPICES:				
Worcestershire Sauce	½ t	1 t	1½ t	2½ t
Cajun Seasoning (more if desired)	1 t	1½ t	1 T	2 T
Tabasco Sauce, to taste				
Black Pepper, to taste				

VARIATIONS AND COMMENTS
Any fresh seafood is a great addition, but shrimp is traditional. Substitute wine or beer for the water.

R

I

C

E

MANDARIN CHICKEN STIR-FRY

A wickedly good, healthy meal that you will be hard pressed to beat by dining out.

AT HOME
Rinse boneless and skinless chicken breast. Cut into strips and put into zip-seal plastic bag with marinade. Freeze at least 24 hours in advance.

IN CAMP
Prep time: 30 minutes / two pots

In a large pot, sauté dry Basmati rice in a little olive oil until it begins to brown. Add water and bring to a boil. Cover and simmer for 20 minutes. Take off heat. While rice is cooking, heat a second pot and toast almonds for two minutes. Remove almonds. Add olive oil, onions, peppers, garlic, and rosemary. Sauté for two minutes. Add thawed chicken and marinade. Stir-fry mixture for 5 minutes. Toss in pea pods; let sit for two minutes on medium heat. Add oranges just before spooning over steaming plates of rice. Garnish with toasted almonds.

Shopping List:	Number of Campers			
	2	**4**	**6**	**12**
Basmati Rice, white	½ c	1 c	1½ c	3 c
Onion, diced	½ c	1 c	1½ c	2½ c
Red Bell Pepper, diced	½	1	2	3
Chicken Breast	8 oz	16 oz	1½ lb	2½ lb
Snow Pea Pods	2 oz	4 oz	6 oz	10 oz
Mandarin Oranges (canned or fresh)	1	1	2	3
Almonds, slivered	1 oz	2 oz	3 oz	5 oz
Garlic Cloves, minced	3	4	6	12
MARINADE:				
Soy Sauce	1 oz	2 oz	3 oz	4 oz
White Wine	1 oz	2 oz	3 oz	4 oz
Worcestershire Sauce	1 t	2 t	3 t	4 t
Ginger, fresh, chopped	½ t	1 t	1½ t	2 t
Rosemary	¼ t	½ t	1 t	2 t
Cracked Black Pepper, to taste				

VARIATIONS AND COMMENTS
Substitute cashews for almonds and broccoli for pea pods—or use them all.

R

I

C

E

CAJUN SEAFOOD IN SAUCE PIQUANTE

A spicy entree from bayou country that will please those that like it hot!

AT HOME

Peel and de-vein shrimp. Place in a zip-seal bag and add enough water to cover them. Freeze. Pack all dry ingredients together and pack fresh veggies in mesh bags so they can breathe.

IN CAMP

Prep time: 40 minutes / two pots

In a large pot, sauté dry Basmati rice in a little olive oil until it begins to brown. Add water and bring to a boil. Cover and simmer for 15 minutes. While rice is cooking, in a second pot, sauté onions, garlic, and peppers in olive oil for approximately 3 minutes. Add 2 t of flour and brown to make a roux. Add tomatoes, corn with water, and seasonings. Cover and simmer for 15 minutes; add thawed shrimp. Cover and simmer another 8 minutes. Adjust spices to taste. Serve on top of rice.

Shopping List:	Number of Campers			
	2	4	6	12
Basmati Rice, white	½ c	1 c	1½ c	3 c
Onion, diced	½	1	2	3
Green Pepper, diced	½	1	2	3
Flour, white unbleached	2 t	2 t	2 t	2 t
Shrimp	8 oz	16 oz	1½ lb	2½ lb
Tomatoes, canned diced	15 oz	24 oz	32 oz	48 oz
Yellow Corn, canned	4-6 oz	15 oz	24 oz	32 oz
Garlic Cloves, minced	4	6	8	16

HERBS AND SPICES:

Prudhomme's Cajun Seafood Seasoning to taste, be generous

Tabasco Sauce, to taste

Cracked Black Pepper, to taste

VARIATIONS AND COMMENTS

Substitute crab or fresh fish for the shrimp. You can also use canned shrimp with pretty good results. This is also great with diced yams tossed into the sauce during the initial sauté.

R

I

C

E

MONGOLIAN BEEF

Whether you think of this as Asian food or not, it doesn't matter. It is fresh, has great textures, and is delicious.

AT HOME
Clean and slice boneless top round or flank steak into small strips. Place in a zip-seal bag and add the marinade. Freeze solid. Make sure vegetables are kept whole and in a breathable bag.

IN CAMP
Prep time: 30 minutes / two pots

In a large pot, sauté dry Basmati rice in a little olive oil until it begins to brown. Add water and bring to a boil. Cover and simmer for 15 minutes. Turn off the heat and let stand covered until the stir-fry mixture is ready. In a second pot, brown the beef and garlic in a touch of olive oil on medium-high heat. Add the veggies and stir-fry for10 minutes. Add marinade, reduce heat, cover, and simmer for 5 minutes. Serve over steaming rice.

Shopping List:	Number of Campers			
	2	4	6	12
Basmati Rice, white	½ c	1 c	1½ c	3 c
Round Steak, thinly sliced	10 oz	20 oz	2 lbs	3½ lbs
Sweet Onion, chopped	1	2	3	5
Red bell pepper, diced	½	2	3	5
Garlic Cloves, minced	2	4	6	12
Scallions (tops and bottoms), diced	3	6	9	18
Carrots, thinly sliced on an angle	2	4	6	12
MARINADE:				
Worcestershire Sauce	1 T	1½ T	2 T	3 T
Soy Sauce	2 T	¼ c	½ c	1 c
Red Wine	2 T	¼ c	½ c	1 c
Smoke Flavor (liquid)	½ t	1 t	1½ t	2 t
Fresh Ginger Root, peeled and chopped	1 t	2 t	1 T	2 T
Black Pepper, to taste				

VARIATIONS AND COMMENTS
This is another I'd-eat-this-at-home favorite among my clients. For two other options you can substitute pork tenderloin or chicken breast for the beef. To eliminate one pan, instead of serving this dish with rice use warmed flour tortillas and serve as a wrap.

R
I
C
E

KICKIN' VEGGIE STEW

This is a terrific vegetarian main dish that can also be served as an excellent cold side salad.

AT HOME
If you are using freeze-dried corn and dried cooked black beans, package them with the spices and dried tomatoes.

IN CAMP
Prep time: 30 minutes / one pot

In a large pot, sauté garlic, onions, and peppers in olive oil on medium heat for two minutes. Add corn (with juice), tomatoes, black beans, and diced sweet potato. Stir. Add seasonings (cumin, Cajun spice, Worcestershire sauce, lime juice, and red pepper sauce); bring to a boil. Reduce heat and simmer covered for 20 minutes. Serve with tortillas to scoop with and dip in the spicy sauce.

Shopping List:	Number of Campers			
	2	4	6	12
Tomatoes, canned diced	15 oz	24 oz	30 oz	60 oz
Black Beans, canned, drained & rinsed	15 oz	24 oz	30 oz	60 oz
Garlic Cloves, minced				
Yellow Corn, canned	15 oz	15 oz	30 oz	48 oz
Onion, chopped	½ c	1 c	1½ c	3 c
Sweet Potato, diced	½ c	1 c	1½ c	3 c
Red or Green Bell Pepper, chopped	½ c	1 c	1½ c	3 c
Limes, for juice	1	2	3	4
HERBS AND SPICES:				
Cajun Spice	½ t	1 t	1½ t	2 t
Worcestershire Sauce	½ t	1 t	1½ t	2 t
Cumin	¼ t	½ t	¾ t	1½ t
Red Pepper Sauce, to taste				

L
E
G
U
M
E
S

VARIATIONS AND COMMENTS
You can make this meal compact and lightweight for backpacking by using dried veggies, but the sweet potatoes will add weight. If you aren't restricted and can use dairy products, serve with a dollop of sour cream on top or softened cream cheese blended with cilantro and garlic. I often pack fresh cilantro and basil in the top of my cheater pack to add a fresh taste to meals.

LENTIL BBQ

You can serve this in a bun, Sloppy Joe style, or ladle it over rice for a really hearty vegetarian meal that will even satisfy carnivores. This idea is contributed by Robert Schrack, a kayak instructor I've worked with from Chesapeake Bay.

AT HOME
Package dry ingredients together in a zip seal bag. Package lentils separately in a large freezer bag to accommodate water for soaking.

IN CAMP
Prep time: 40 minutes / one pot

Soak lentils overnight if possible, but 2 hours is sufficient. Drain and rinse. Create BBQ sauce by sautéing vegetables and garlic in olive oil until slightly tender; add tomato sauce, spices, brown sugar and mustard. Stir well while warming through and remove from heat. In another large pot, put lentils in enough water to cover by an inch and bring to a boil. If well-soaked, lentils should be fairly tender after about 20 minutes and most water absorbed. Stir in BBQ sauce mixture and simmer another 10 minutes and serve.

Shopping List:	Number of Campers			
	2	**4**	**6**	**12**
Lentils	1 c	2 c	3 c	5 c
Water	3 c	5 c	7 c	12 c
Onion, chopped	1 c	1 c	1½ c	3 c
Bell Pepper, chopped	1 c	1 c	1½ c	3 c
Garlic, Cloves, minced	3	5	8	12
Tomato Sauce	6oz	12 oz	16 oz	32 oz
HERBS AND SPICES:				
Worcestershire Sauce	1 t	2 t	1 T	2 T
Brown Sugar or Honey	1T	2T	3T	1c
Mustard	2 t	1T	2 T	1/2c
Red Pepper Sauce, to taste	¼ t	½ t	1 t	2 t
Oregano	½ t	1 t	2 t	3 t
Thyme	¼ t	½ t	1 t	2 t
Black Pepper, to taste				

L
E
G
U
M
E
S

VARIATIONS AND COMMENTS
Try serving this over freshly baked slabs of cornbread!

MEDITERRANEAN LENTIL STEW

This is a hearty soup with deep flavors that vegans and carnivores alike will appreciate. It can be prepared with all fresh ingredients, wine, and olives for home use and paddling trips. For a lighter-weight option, it works well with dried vegetables.

AT HOME

For lightweight version, chop sun-dried tomatoes and combine all dry ingredients, including the lentils, in a zip-seal plastic bag.

IN CAMP
Prep time: 50 minutes / one pot

For the light version, add water to the zip-seal bag of dry ingredients and soak for a minimum of two hours to overnight (easy). In a large pot, sauté garlic on medium heat in olive oil for 5 minutes. Add bagged contents, spices, water enough to cover and bring to a boil. Lower heat and simmer until lentils are tender. You may need to add water during the simmering process to get proper consistency of the lentils. More simmer time results in deeper flavors.

Warm chocolate cake.

L
E
G
U
M
E
S

Shopping List:	Number of Campers			
	2	**4**	**6**	**12**
Lentils	1 c	2 c	3 c	5 c

FOR THE LIGHTWEIGHT VERSION PACK THESE WITH THE LENTILS:

Onion, dried flakes	1 T	2 T	3 T	½ c
Bell Peppers, dried and chopped	1 T	2 T	3 T	½ c
Sun-dried Tomatoes, chopped	¼ c	1/3 c	¾ c	1 c

ADD THE FOLLOWING INGREDIENTS:

Garlic Cloves, minced	3	5	8	12
Water	3 c	5 c	7 c	12 c
Black Olives, canned and chopped	2 oz	2 oz	4 oz	8 oz

FOR THE FRESH VERSION, SAUTÉ THE FOLLOWING WITH THE GARLIC:

Garlic Cloves, minced	3	5	8	12
Onion, chopped	1 c	1 c	1½ c	3 c
Bell Pepper, chopped	1 c	1 c	1½ c	3 c

AFTER SAUTÉING THE ABOVE, ADD:

Tomatoes, canned and diced	15 oz	15 oz	30 oz	50 oz
Dry Red Wine (or vegetable broth or water)	2½ c	4 c	6 c	3 qts
Black Olives, canned and chopped	2 oz	2 oz	4 oz	8 oz

HERBS AND SPICES:

Worcestershire Sauce	1 t	2 t	1 T	2 T
Balsamic Vinegar	1 T	1½ T	2 T	3 T
Bay Leaves	1	2	3	3
Basil	½ t	1 t	2 t	3 t
Oregano	½ t	1 t	2 t	3 t
Thyme	¼ t	½ t	1 t	2 t
Red Pepper Sauce, to taste				
Black Pepper, to taste				

VARIATIONS AND COMMENTS

For a fresh version, soak uncooked lentils overnight (can use half sea water) and rinse. Red wine adds richness and can be used in any combination with the broth or water to get the right amount of liquid.

L
E
G
U
M
E
S

MEATY VEGETARIAN CHILI

Whether served with cornbread dumplings or tortillas, this is one crowd-pleasing pot full of flavor that is super-easy to make.

AT HOME
Combine all dry ingredients, including spices and herbs, in a zip-seal plastic bag.

IN CAMP
Prep time: 25 minutes / one pot

Empty the bag of ingredients into a large pot. Add the water and bring to a boil. Add Worcestershire sauce and red pepper sauce. Reduce heat and simmer for 20 minutes.

L
E
G
U
M
E
S

Fantastic Foods brand instant beans are often found in supermarkets in the same aisle as couscous or other international foods. Another great product called "Fiesta Beans" is available from restaurant supply stores like Gordon Food Service. Try your local food co-op as a source for quality dried pre-cooked bean mixes. If using the Fantastic Foods brand, don't use as much water as directed as it will turn out too thin.

Shopping List:	Number of Campers			
	2	**4**	**6**	**12**
Instant Refried Beans (boxes) Fantastic Foods brand works well	½	1	1½	3
Bulgur Wheat ("cracked" wheat)	½ c	¾ c	1 c	2 c
Dried Onions	1 T	1½ T	2 T	¼ c
Dried Bell Peppers	1 T	2 T	3 T	½ c
Freeze-dried Yellow Corn	1 T	2 T	3 T	½ c
Garlic, dried, chopped	1 t	2 t	1 T	2 T
Sun-dried Tomatoes, chopped	½ c	¾ c	1 c	2 c
Water	3 c	5 c	7 c	12 c
HERBS AND SPICES:				
Worcestershire Sauce	1 t	2 t	1 T	2 T
Bay Leaves	1	2	3	3
Basil	½ t	1 t	2 t	3 t
Oregano	½ t	1 t	2 t	3 t
Coriander	¼ t	½ t	1 t	2 t
Cumin	1½ t	1 T	1½ T	3 T
Chili Powder	1½ t	1 T	1½ T	3 T
Red Pepper sauce, to taste				
Black Pepper, to taste				

VARIATIONS AND COMMENTS

I'd put this up against any prepared product for taste and portability. You may need to add more water during the simmering process to get proper consistency. If you are unfamiliar with bulgur, it's the wheat base for Tabouli and can be found in bulk at food co-ops. It is also good with sliced carrots, canned tomatoes and canned beans if you aren't weight restricted. A small can of tomato paste adds richness. If you have a covered pot with an inch and a half or more of headroom between the chili and the lid, you can make cornbread dumplings (see page 73) during the last 10 minutes of cooking to get two dishes from one pot. Now, that's magic.

L

E

G

U

M

E

S

WHITE-BEAN CHICKEN CHILI

This yields a rich tasty meal that everyone seems to like right down to the five year olds.

AT HOME

Put all dry ingredients in a zip-seal bag. Store near the canned ingredients in a stuff sack.

IN CAMP

Prep time: 25 minutes / one pot

In a large pot, sauté garlic and onions in olive oil until the onion is tender. Add everything else (do not drain beans); bring to a boil and stir. Reduce heat, cover, and simmer for about 10 minutes. Gently stir cream cheese into the sauce.

Shopping List:	Number of Campers			
	2	4	6	12
White Beans (any kind) 15 oz can	1	2	3	4
White Chicken Meat, 6 oz can or foil pouch	1 pkg	2 pkg	2 pkg	4 pkg
Cream Cheese (Neufchatel works)	4 oz	6 oz	8 oz	16 oz
Onion, diced	½ c	1 c	1½ c	2½ c
Salsa	4 oz	8 oz	12 oz	16 oz
Water	1c	2c	3c	6c
HERBS AND SPICES:				
Cumin	1 t	2 t	1 T	2 T
Chili Powder	1 t	2 t	1 T	2 T
Red Pepper Sauce, to taste				
Black Pepper, to taste				
Salt, to taste				

VARIATIONS AND COMMENTS

You may need to add a bit more water during the cooking process to get the desired thickness. Although not a lightweight meal choice, this one satisfies most palates and is so easy to make that your kids could make it after school and have it ready when you get home. Hmm, now there's an idea. Great served with a Quesadilla appetizer, cornbread, or with chunks of hearty whole-grain bread. If you use a dry salsa mix, then add a can of diced tomatoes for moisture.

L
E
G
U
M
E
S

BEAN BURRITOS

When you are hungry NOW, this hearty and easy-to-prepare meal remains one of our favorites for a satisfying dinner.

AT HOME
Store bean mix, cumin, and dried onion in a zip-seal plastic bag.

IN CAMP
Prep time: 10 minutes / one pot

In a large pot, add the bean mix, water (amount as directed on the mix), and Worcestershire sauce. Bring to a boil while stirring occasionally. Cover and remove from heat. Let stand for a few minutes. While this sits to thicken, slice up some sharp cheddar cheese and warm the tortillas. Wrap some cheese and the burrito mix in large flour tortillas. You can add spice with some canned or reconstituted dried salsa, or for a real bonanza, smother the burritos with sun-dried tomato salsa.

Shopping List:	Number of Campers			
	2	**4**	**6**	**12**
Onion, dried	1 oz	2 oz	3 oz	5 oz
Instant Refried Bean mix*, 5 oz box	1	2	3	4
Flour Tortillas	4	8	12	24
Cheddar Cheese, sliced	4 oz	8 oz	12 oz	24 oz
HERBS AND SPICES:				
Worcestershire Sauce	½ t	1 t	1½ t	2½ t
Cumin	1 t	1½ t	1 T	2 T
Black Pepper, to taste				

VARIATIONS AND COMMENTS
*Fantastic Foods brand instant beans are often found in supermarkets in the same aisle as couscous or other international foods. Another great product called "Fiesta Beans" is available from restaurant supply stores like Gordon Food Service. Try your local food co-op as a source for quality dried pre-cooked bean mixes. If using the Fantastic Foods brand, don't add as much water as directed as it will turn out too thin.

L
E
G
U
M
E
S

SUN-DRIED TOMATO SALSA

Serve hot over just about anything; you will definitely want to start making this at home—it's that good.

AT HOME

Chop sun-dried tomatoes and mix with the other ingredients in a zip-seal bag. Kitchen shears work very well to cut these leathery little buggers.

IN CAMP

Prep time: 15 minutes / one pot

Pour contents into a pot, cover with an inch of water, add Worcestershire Sauce, and bring to a boil. Simmer until it reaches a uniform consistency.

Shopping List:	Number of Campers			
	2	**4**	**6**	**12**
Sun-dried Tomatoes, finely chopped	1 oz	2 oz	3 oz	6 oz
Dried Onions, diced	1 oz	2 oz	3 oz	5 oz
Dried Bell Peppers, chopped	1 oz	2 oz	3 oz	5 oz
Dried Chipotle Peppers, chopped	1	2	3	4
Garlic, dried, chopped	½ t	1 t	1½ t	2 t
HERBS AND SPICES:				
Worcestershire Sauce	½ t	1 t	1½ t	2½ t
Cumin	1 t	1½ t	1 T	2 T
Black Pepper, to taste				

VARIATIONS AND COMMENTS

Substitute chipotle sauce for whole peppers (Bufalo Chipotle Hot Sauce rocks). Use red pepper flakes instead of chipotles if you don't want a smoky flavor. This sauce is also great in quesadillas, on enchilada pie, or on chicken tacos. If your taste buds prefer the milder side, simply use a small squirt of Chipotle in the tomato mixture and they will be happy.

L
E
G
U
M
E
S

ENCHILADA PIE

Sometimes the sense of community and enjoyment that comes from serving everyone out of one big fragrant pot simply cannot be duplicated. This is one such meal.

AT HOME

Combine dry bean mix, spices, and dried veggies together in a zip-seal plastic bag.

IN CAMP

Prep time: 30 minutes / two pots

Combine the dry bean mix, veggie and spice mix with Worcestershire sauce and water (as directed on package). Bring to a boil while stirring occasionally. Cover and remove from heat. Let stand for several minutes for the beans to thicken. Then, using a large pot or Dutch oven, layer the following ingredients: large flour tortillas, the thickened bean mixture, grated cheddar or jack cheese, salsa, and canned yellow corn until you have two layers of each, ending with tortilla layer on top. You may have enough components for a third layer—go for it. The larger the group, the larger the pot and the deeper the pie grows. Cover the pot and let it sit on low heat for 15 to 20 minutes to melt the cheese and allow the flavors to mingle.

Shopping List:	Number of Campers			
	2	4	6	12
*Pre-cooked Dry Bean Mix	6 oz	12 oz	1 lb	2 lbs
Onion, dry	½	1	2	3
Red or Green Pepper, dry	½	1	2	3
Cheese, Jack or Cheddar, grated	4 oz	8 oz	12 oz	16 oz
Yellow Corn, canned, drained	4 oz	8 oz	12 oz	16 oz
Salsa, small tin	4 oz	8 oz	12 oz	16 oz
Flour Tortillas, burrito size	3	3	6	10
HERBS AND SPICES:				
Cumin	1 t	1½ t	1 T	2 T
Black Pepper, to taste				

VARIATIONS AND COMMENTS

For added protein, add canned chicken to the salsa layer. The small tins of salsa come in several varieties; some are hotter than others. This recipe works great with canned Mexican Salsa Ranchera.

*Fantastic Foods brand instant beans are often found in supermarkets in the same aisle as couscous or other international foods. Another great product called "Fiesta Beans" is available from restaurant supply stores. If using the Fantastic Foods brand, don't add as much water as directed as it will turn out too thin.

L
E
G
U
M
E
S

117

CHICKEN AND BLACK-BEAN BURRITOS

You can use all sorts of beans and you don't need to worry about using exact amounts of corn or beans—be fearless.

AT HOME

Combine the dry bean mix, cumin, chili powder, black pepper, and dried onions in a zip-seal plastic bag.

IN CAMP

Prep time: 10 minutes / one pot

Sauté the corn and onion (if using fresh onion) in a small amount of olive oil on medium heat for two minutes. Add bean/spice mixture and water as directed on the mix. Bring to a boil while stirring. Add canned or pouched chicken. Cover and remove pot from heat. Let stand for a few minutes. While mixture is resting, thinly slice some cheddar cheese. Wrap the cheese and the thickened bean mixture in flour tortillas. Add salsa or your favorite chili sauce.

Shopping List:	Number of Campers			
	2	**4**	**6**	**12**
Yellow Corn, canned (drained)	15 oz	30 oz	45 oz	5 lbs
Onion (fresh), chopped	½	1	2	3
or Onion (dried)	1 oz	2 oz	3 oz	5 oz
Instant Black Beans (6 oz box)	1	2	3	4
(Fantastic Foods brand)				
or Black Beans (canned), drained	10 oz	20 oz	30 oz	4 lbs
Chicken, canned or foil pouch	6 oz	12 oz	18 oz	36 oz
Flour Tortillas	4	8	12	24
Cheddar Cheese, sliced	4 oz	8 oz	12 oz	24 oz
HERBS AND SPICES:				
Cumin	1 t	1½ t	1 T	2 T
Chili Powder	1 t	1½ t	1 T	2 T
Black Pepper, to taste				

L
E
G
U
M
E
S

VARIATIONS AND COMMENTS

You can make this a lightweight meal for backpacking by using only dried ingredients. Freeze-dried corn and dehydrated chicken work well and taste good. For paddling trips, I use all canned ingredients. Try your local food co-op as a source for quality dried and pre-cooked bean mixes. There is also a product called "Fiesta Beans" found in restaurant supply stores that is good. If using Fantastic Foods brand, don't add as much water as directed as it will turn out too thin.

CUBAN BLACK BEANS AND YELLOW RICE

Eleven seasons of guiding in south Florida waters has produced this hearty vegetarian entrée with roots in the Cuban cantinas of the Conch Republic. It is easy, lightweight, and satisfying.

AT HOME
If using dried black bean mix, store in a zip-seal plastic bag so it doesn't escape.

IN CAMP
Prep time: 25 minutes / two pots

In one pot, boil water for rice. Once the water boils add rice, cover, and cook according to the mix directions. While the rice is cooking, heat a little olive oil in a large pot and sauté onions, peppers, and garlic on medium heat for two minutes. Add the bean mix and water as directed on the mix, Worcestershire sauce, Balsamic vinegar, and seasonings. Cover and simmer until rice is done. Serve over steaming rice.

Shopping List:	Number of Campers			
	2	**4**	**6**	**12**
Yellow Rice Mix, Vigo brand	6 oz	12 oz	18 oz	32 oz
Onion, diced	½	1	2	3
Red or Green Pepper, diced	½	1	2	3
Pre-cooked Dry Bean Mix (6 oz box) *Fantastic Foods brand is preferred*	1	2	3	4
Garlic Cloves, minced	3	4	6	12
HERBS AND SPICES:				
Worcestershire Sauce	½ t	1 t	1½ t	2½ t
Balsamic Vinegar	½ t	1 t	1½ t	2½ t
Cajun Seasoning	1 t	1½ t	1 T	2 T
Black Pepper, to taste				

L
E
G
U
M
E
S

VARIATIONS AND COMMENTS
Add smoked sausage to bean mixture. Substitute other brands of dried black beans or use canned beans if weight is not an issue. This is also a fantastic side dish to serve with freshly caught fish!

HOPPIN' JOHN

While canoeing around some islands in the Gulf of Mexico, I met a couple from the state of Georgia who introduced me to the secrets of black-eyed peas. Don't freak over the anchovies, they are the secret ingredient that makes this meal so good.

AT HOME

Package the dry ingredients together and make sure the fresh veggies are stored in a mesh bag so they can breathe.

IN CAMP

Prep time: 60 minutes / one pot

Start with the basic four food groups—garlic, peppers, onions, and olive oil—in the bottom of your pot. Sauté veggies for a couple of minutes, then add everything except the uncooked rice. Bring to a boil, reduce heat, cover, and simmer for 30 minutes. Add the rice, stir, and cover. Let this simmer another 20 minutes. When the beans are soft enough for your tastes, the meal is ready to be served.

Shopping List:	Number of Campers			
	2	4	6	12
Black-eyed Peas, uncooked	1 c	2 c	3 c	6 c
Rice, uncooked	1/3 c	2/3 c	1 c	2 c
Spanish Onion, chopped	½ c	1 c	2 c	3 c
Red or Green Pepper, diced	½ c	1 c	2 c	3 c
Anchovy Paste (or canned whole anchovies)	2 t	1 T	1½ T	3 T
Garlic Cloves, minced	3	4	6	12
HERBS AND SPICES:				
Worcestershire Sauce	1 t	2 t	1 T	2 T
Soy Sauce	1 t	2 t	1 T	2 T
Red Pepper sauce	1 t	2 t	1 T	2 T
Black Pepper, to taste				

L
E
G
U
M
E
S

VARIATIONS AND COMMENTS

Smoked sausage is a flavorful addition. You can give a Creole jolt by adding Cajun spices and more pepper sauce, if you like. This is a hearty dish that you will get amazing mileage out of.

FALAFEL POCKETS

Dried falafel mix is lightweight, tasty, and packs a wallop in both the heartiness and flatulence categories. Consequently it is great for cooler weather when your tent is cold and your nose is already running.

AT HOME
Package dry mix in a watertight container and be sure fresh veggies are in a breathable mesh bag.

IN CAMP
Prep time: 15 minutes / frying pan

In a bowl combine water and falafel mix according to directions (about 20 minutes early to allow full hydration). While the mix is hydrating you can chop the cucumbers, parsley, onion, and tomatoes to sandwich-topping size. In a frying pan that is heated and lightly oiled, pat out spoonfuls of the falafel mix into 1- to 2-inch patties (you don't have to deep fry them). Turn the patties after a couple of minutes and brown on the other side. You can warm pita halves on top of the cooking falafel patties. Mix chopped veggies with plain yogurt or tadziki dressing. Stuff a few patties into the pita pocket bread (or tortillas); top with vegetable mixture and more dressing if desired.

Shopping List:	Number of Campers			
	2	**4**	**6**	**12**
Falafel Mix, dry	½ c	1 c	2 c	4 c
Sweet Onion, baseball sized, diced	½	1	2	3
Cucumber, diced	1	2	3	6
Tomato, diced	1	2	3	6
Parsley, fresh, chopped	¼ c	½ c	1 c	2 c
Pita Bread, cut in halves	3	6	12	24
Plain Yogurt or Prepared Tadziki sauce	½ c	1 c	1 c	2 c

HERBS AND SPICES:
Most dry falafel mixes come pre-seasoned. They're most often found in food co-ops in box or bulk.

VARIATIONS AND COMMENTS
These pockets are good topped with grated cheddar cheese, or the Greek Cabbage Salad, or Crunchy Cabbage & Apple Salad, or a Tabouli salad made from a dry mix. If you are making Tabouli from a dry mix, be sure to bring a couple of lemons. Fresh lemon juice improves the Tabouli immensely. Hummus makes a nice appetizer for this meal. These pockets are easy to make and they taste more like I'd-eat-this-anywhere rather than trail food. Prepared yogurt, tadziki sauce, and ranch dressing work well for toppings and will keep fine until opened. Buy small containers or use your soft-sided cooler.

L
E
G
U
M
E
S

Leaky Kayaks, Kiwis, and Random Events

While teaching an outdoor cooking course for Nelson, New Zealand's Polytech, I made friends with Ian. We met when he came out to paddle the coast of Abel Tasman National Park where I was living in a tent at the end of the Abel Tasman Track. Later, I ran into him at random strolls down the sidewalk in Nelson, an hour's travel away. Still later, after a rigorous solo backpack along the Pelorus River, I was unsuccessfully trying to hitch the sixty miles back to Nelson when a bus pulled over. The driver's window slid open to reveal a shouted, "Michael, you shaved your beard!" Ian, driving the bus, said to me, "You know what this means? We have to do a paddle trip!"

After I climbed in and settled into the seat behind him, I asked when he could leave. Ian said, "Well, I'll have to quit my job."

"Is that a problem?" I asked.

"Naw, give me two weeks," was his simple reply. And over the next hour of bumpy road we made an ambitious plan to meet up on Stewart Island in the Southern Ocean between the South Island of New Zealand and Antarctica.

Some of the best expeditions are planned on the back of cocktail napkins and this proved to be no exception. We showed up on the island independently within a day of each other with our hastily packed supplies. After trying to glean some local knowledge from the odd lot of residents and a serious phone conversation with

Paul Caffyn (Kiwi explorer who had circumnavigated Stewart Island), Ian and I opted for an exploration of Patterson Inlet's more sheltered waters. That seemed like good judgement, given that the waves were ranging five to eight on the exposed coast … meters. Two weeks prior, our food "planning" went like this: "You bring a kilo of rice and cheese; I'll bring flour, tea and sugar." Once re-united over Steinlagers at the local pub, we surveyed our communal supplies and discovered we also had onions, yeast, and garlic. "Well, mate, we can go for two weeks if we want with this lot."

So, off we went in a borrowed plastic Puffin kayak and Ian's old fiberglass kayak, the Orange Roughy. We supplemented our diet with mussels, blue cod, and the occasional dinner-plate sized scallop. Our best meal was a wonderful seafood stew into which we dipped crusty French bread that we baked in an old coffee can we found, cut the bottom out of and rolled around on the coals of a fire. This came at the end of a ten-hour paddling day into headwinds and relentless rain. I peered at Ian's kayak through the gloom and said, "Ian, you're sinking."

He looked at me and agreed, "I reckon, shall we go to land?" After nearly giving ourselves double hernias, we hoisted the waterlogged kayak up onto the cobble beach above the high tide line.

"Shouldn't we dump it out?" I asked.

Ian replied, "It's on land now. The water will go out the same holes that it came in."

CHICKEN STEW WITH DUMPLINGS

This comfort food will warm your belly on a cool evening. It's a family favorite.

AT HOME

Package the produce loosely in a mesh bag (onion sacks work well). Watch for amounts of MSG (monosodium glutamate) in soup bases. It doesn't get along well with some people's systems.

IN CAMP
Prep time: 50 minutes / one pot

Chop the raw vegetables into bite-size pieces. Sauté the vegetables and minced garlic in a touch of olive oil in the bottom of a large pot. When everything starts to brown, slowly add water, the soup base, chicken, and spices. Bring to a boil. Reduce heat and cover. Simmer for 25 minutes. Mix a little water with flour or biscuit mix in a cup to make a thickening paste; stir into the stew until the broth thickens to desired consistency. Add dumpling dough (see recipe on page 73) and cover. Simmer another 10 minutes or until dumplings are done. Don't panic. Even if you think you goofed, it will taste good.

Chicken Recipes

These meals can be prepared with canned or pouched chicken or fresh chicken breasts you've cleaned, marinated, and frozen at home. If you use the latter, the meat should be kept in a cooler for a nice meal on night one or two of your trip. You can pre-cook your own chicken if you are going to use it early in the trip and have a small cooler.

C
H
I
C
K
E
N

Shopping List:	Number of Campers			
	2	**4**	**6**	**12**
Red Potatoes, quartered, golf-ball size	3	6	9	16
Carrots, regular size	1	2	3	6
Onion, tangerine size	1	2	3	5
Chicken, canned	6 oz	12 oz	18 oz	32 oz
Garlic Cloves, minced	3	4	6	12
Water	2 c	3 c	4 c	8 c
HERBS AND SPICES:				
Dry Chicken Soup base	1 t	2 t	1 T	2 T
Worcestershire Sauce	1 t	2 t	1 T	2 T
Soy Sauce	1 t	2 t	1 T	2 T
Basil, dry	1 t	2 t	1 T	2 T
Oregano, dry	½ t	1 t	2 t	1 T
Black Pepper, to taste				

VARIATIONS AND COMMENTS

The soy sauce will provide enough saltiness. You may need to add more water to get the right consistency. Canned turkey or canned beef can be substituted for the chicken.

Sometimes Mother Nature provides dessert, like this pot of freshly picked blueberries found near Lake Superior in Northern Michigan.

CHICKEN FAJITAS

No one has ever complained about eating this well in the wild. This is quick to prepare for a hungry crowd.

AT HOME

This is one of those "cheater meals" where you need a small cooler to keep the chicken, fresh veggies, and herbs lively for a couple of days. Mix marinade ingredients in a heavy-duty, zip-seal plastic bag. Rinse skinless, boneless chicken breast. Cut into thin slices and add to the marinade. Freeze hard as a rock. Pack veggies in breathable mesh bags. Store fresh cilantro on top of cooler.

IN CAMP
Prep time: 20 minutes / one pot

Sauté thawed chicken in olive oil for a few minutes. Add the thawed marinade and coarsely chopped peppers and onions. Cover and simmer for 10 minutes. Turn down the heat and warm tortillas on top of the pot. While the meal simmers, chop tomatoes, garlic, chilies, and cilantro; add freshly squeezed lime juice to make Pico de Gallo fresh salsa. Next finely chop or shred the cheese. To serve, simply make it buffet style and have each person spoon a little of each into a warmed 6- to 8-inch flour tortilla.

Shopping List:	Number of Campers			
	2	4	6	12
Chicken Breast, in strips	12 oz	24 oz	2 lbs	4 lbs
Sweet Onion, (tangerine sized)	1	2	3	5
Green Pepper	1	2	3	5
Garlic Cloves	1	2	3	4
Tomatoes (can be canned diced)	1	2	3	5
Chilies (Jalapenos, add more if you like fire)	1	2	3	5
Cilantro, fresh	1 T	2 T	3 T	4 T
Limes	1	2	3	5
Cheddar Cheese	4 oz	6 oz	8 oz	1 lbs
Flour Tortillas (6" to 8")	6	12	18	36
MARINADE INGREDIENTS:				
Worcestershire Sauce	1 T	1½ T	2 T	3 T
Soy Sauce	1 T	1½ T	2 T	3 T
Beer or Red Wine	¼ c	1/3 c	½ c	1 c
Smoke Flavor (liquid)	¼ t	½ t	½ t	1 t
Cumin (ground)	½ t	1 t	1½ t	2 t
Black Pepper, to taste				

VARIATIONS AND COMMENTS
Substitute beef for the chicken or canned tomatoes and chilies for fresh. Try with our Sun-dried tomato salsa in place of the Pico de Gallo.

C
H
I
C
K
E
N

CHICKEN TACOS

A super-speedy, lightweight crowd pleaser that makes its way onto our menu two out of three trips.

AT HOME
Depending on any weight restrictions, you can use dried ingredients or pack the fresh veggies in mesh bags so they can breathe.

IN CAMP
Prep time: 10 minutes / one pot

In a large pot, sauté onions and peppers in a small amount of olive oil on medium heat for two minutes. Add canned chicken, salsa, and herbs and spices. Stir while heating for a few minutes until heated through. Fold into fajita-size flour tortillas with grated cheddar cheese. Serve with Crunchy Cabbage & Apple Salad or Gonzo Rice.

Shopping List:	Number of Campers			
	2	**4**	**6**	**12**
Chicken (6 oz can)	1	2	3	6
Onion, diced	½ c	1 c	2 c	3 c
Bell Peppers, diced	½ c	1 c	2 c	3 c
Salsa	2 oz	4 oz	6 oz	12 oz
Cheddar Cheese, shredded	2 oz	4 oz	6 oz	12 oz
Flour Tortillas (6" to 8")	6	12	18	36
LIGHTWEIGHT DRY OPTIONS:				
Onion Flakes	1 oz	2 oz	3 oz	5 oz
Bell Peppers	1 oz	2 oz	3 oz	5 oz
Salsa can be dried as well				
HERBS AND SPICES:				
Worcestershire Sauce	½ t	1 t	1½ t	2½ t
Cumin	1 t	1½ t	1 T	2 T
Black Pepper, to taste				

VARIATIONS AND COMMENTS
For backpacking trips or long-distance tours where lightness is a huge benefit, use dried vegetables and dried salsa.

C
H
I
C
K
E
N

127

CHICKEN AND GRAVY

Pure comfort food when served with Garlic Smashed Spuds.

AT HOME
Package with your mashed potato kit.

IN CAMP
Prep time: 15 minutes / one pot

In a large pot, make a good-quality chicken gravy mix according to the package directions. Add the canned white chicken; add herbs and spices. Warm through on low heat and serve over the Garlic Smashed Spuds.

Shopping List:	Number of Campers			
	2	**4**	**6**	**12**
Chicken (8 oz can)	1	2	3	6
Gravy Mix (look for brands without MSG)	1 pkt	1 pkt	2 pkt	3 pkt
HERBS AND SPICES:				
Worcestershire Sauce	1 t	1½ t	2 t	1 T
Black Pepper, to taste				

VARIATIONS AND COMMENTS
Try sautéing a bit of onion in the pot prior to adding the gravy and meat. The onion, along with the Worcestershire sauce, will take away the tinny taste. If you can find canned turkey, feel free to substitute for the chicken. If you add a little instant stuffing you have Sunday dinner!

C
H
I
C
K
E
N

PAN-SEARED PORK TENDERLOIN IN CHERRY RED-WINE PEPPERCORN SAUCE

This hearty dish is worth the effort and will please even the most devout carnivores.

AT HOME

Prepare marinade and pour it into a zip-seal bag. Put the whole pork tenderloin into it. Squeeze out excess air and freeze solid.

IN CAMP

Prep time: 30 minutes / one frying pan, one pot

Remove the thawed tenderloin from the bag. Drain the meat, but reserve marinade. Coat bottom of a frying pan with olive oil and heat until just about smoking. Sear the meat on high heat in the frying pan for 5 minutes or so. Sear all sides. Reduce flame to medium-low and cover. Give it 10 minutes, then turn and give it another 10 minutes on the other side.

While the tenderloin is cooking, in a separate pot heat the reserved marinade to a boil. If you are serving a large group add a bit more cracked pepper and red wine. Once a small amount of the marinade is boiled off (hey, you're making a reduction sauce...cool) reduce the heat and add a bit of cornstarch to thicken the marinade to a glaze consistency. Serve it over the sliced meat.

Shopping List:	Number of Campers			
	2	4	6	12
Pork Tenderloin	1 lb	2 lbs	3 lbs	6 lbs
MARINADE INGREDIENTS:				
Dry Red Wine (Cabernet works well)	½ c	½ c	1 c	1½ c
Worcestershire Sauce	1 t	1 t	1 T	2 T
Cherries, dried	½ c	½ c	½ c	½ c
Garlic Cloves, crushed	2	2	3	5
Cracked Peppercorns	1 T	1 T	1½ T	2 T
Thyme	½ t	½ t	1 t	1½ t

VARIATIONS AND COMMENTS

This is terrific paired with Garlic Smashed Spuds and the Crunchy Cabbage & Apple Salad or warm homemade applesauce (which can be made from dried apples). If you really want to go nuts, cook some sliced Portobello mushrooms in the sauce and serve over the sliced pork.

P

O

R

K

TROUT POACHED IN
WHITE WINE AND HERBS

One kayak tour around the southern edge of Isle Royale National Park in Lake Superior produced so many lake trout while we trolled that we got more creative with recipes. This is a quick one that turned out to be a hit.

AT HOME

If you are unable to acquire fresh fish during your trip, then at least 24 hours before your departure, freeze fish filets in a small amount of water in a zip-seal bag—or have a local vendor vacuum-seal the filets for you and then freeze the package. Store the frozen fish in the bottom of your cheater pack.

IN CAMP

Prep time: 15 minutes / one pot

If you are lucky enough to catch fish along the way, keep alive until just before you want to eat, then filet. Arrange the filets in a wide shallow pot that has a tight-fitting lid. Add white wine and lemon juice and sprinkle each filet liberally with herbs. Cover and steam for about 10 minutes or until the fish flakes nicely and is no longer translucent. Easy cooking and easier cleanup!

Shopping List:	Number of Campers			
	2	4	6	12
Fresh Fish, filets	1 lb	2 lbs	3 lbs	6 lbs
Lemon Juice (liquid or fresh)	2 T	3 T	3 T	4 T
White Wine	½ c	¾ c	1 c	1½ c
HERB MIXTURE:				
Basil	pinch	¼ t	½ t	1 t
Oregano	pinch	¼ t	½ t	1 t
Dill	pinch	¼ t	½ t	1 t

VARIATIONS AND COMMENTS

Try this recipe with any kind of fresh fish, although it is not recommended for thin filets. It is especially good with salmon steaks. It is easy to make this meal if you are backpacking—if you catch your fish and use dried lemon peel (or lemon pepper) instead of juice and water instead of wine. When served with soda bread and Greek Cabbage Salad it is a meal that will rival anything you ever had to leave a tip for.

F

I

S

H

ORANGE-HICKORY GRILLED LAKE TROUT

Paddle trips at Isle Royale often end up with a post trip feast at the Harbor Haus in Copper Harbor. After years of taste testing their menu, I've come up with this favorite so you can short cut the process a bit.

AT HOME

If you are unable to acquire fresh fish during your trip, then at least 24 hours before your departure, freeze fish filets in a small amount of water in a zip-seal bag—or have a local vendor vacuum-seal the filets for you and then freeze the package. Store the frozen fish in the bottom of your cheater pack.

IN CAMP
Prep time: 30+ minutes / frying pan or foil

Keep the fish alive and filet just before dinner. To make the glaze, mix honey, freshly squeezed orange juice, grated orange zest (shave the peel with a pocketknife), and spices together. Coat the fish thoroughly with the glaze and let marinate 30 minutes before cooking. This is best cooked over an open fire, but you can use a covered frying pan or griddle on medium heat. If using a pan, cook in covered pan 5 or 6 minutes on each side, turning only once. Hint: always start with the skin side up. Squeeze more orange juice on top of the filets as soon as you put them in the pan and just after the flip to help steam and to avoid sticking. If cooking over an open fire, use perforated foil or a fine-mesh grill. Turn once.

Shopping List:	Number of Campers			
	2	4	6	12
Fresh Fish, filets	1 lb	2 lbs	3 lbs	6 lbs
GLAZE INGREDIENTS:				
Oranges (for fresh juice)	½	1	1½	3
Honey	1 T	2 T	3 T	5 T
Chili Powder	¼ t	½ t	1 t	2 t
Allspice	pinch	¼ t	½ t	1 t
Hickory Smoke, liquid flavor	¼ t	½ t	1t	1 t

VARIATIONS AND COMMENTS

This succulent recipe works with any trout or salmon. It might also be good with grouper or snapper for those venturing into marine environments. Try adding a few hot-pepper flakes to the glaze for a Jamaican influence. Scallions, chives, and garlic are also good if chopped finely and added to the glaze. Serve with cabbage or pasta salad.

F

I

S

H

PARMESAN PEPPERCORN WHITEFISH

Whitefish is a Great Lakes specialty that is terrific when served freshly caught.

AT HOME

If you are unable to acquire fresh fish during your trip, then at least 24 hours before your departure, freeze fish filets in a small amount of water in a zip-seal bag—or have a local vendor vacuum-seal whitefish filets for you and then freeze the package. Store the frozen fish in the bottom of your cheater pack.

IN CAMP

Prep time: 20 minutes / one frying pan

While a small amount of olive oil is heating in the frying pan, mix the coating ingredients. Lay the filets on a plate and dust both sides of each filet with the coating. Gently lay filets into the frying pan. Sauté a few minutes on each side until golden.

Shopping List:	Number of Campers			
	2	4	6	12
Fresh Fish, filets	1 lb	2 lbs	3 lbs	6 lbs
BREADING MIX:				
All-purpose Flour	¼ c	½ c	½ c	1 c
Parmesan Cheese, grated	¼ c	½ c	½ c	1 c
Cracked Pepper	1 T	1½ T	2½ T	4 T
Garlic Powder	¼ t	½ t	¾ t	1½ t

VARIATIONS AND COMMENTS

This breading works equally well with any light-tasting fish, like cod, grouper, and halibut. Try combining this meal with a Greek salad and freshly baked biscuits for a dinner you can serve anywhere to rave reviews.

F

I

S

H

JAMAICAN JERK SALMON

This unique flavor hails from the island of Jamaica and loves to be accompanied by good bread and cold beer.

AT HOME

Mix together the dry herbs and spices; package in a small zip-seal bag. If you are unable to acquire fresh fish during your trip, then at least 24 hours before your departure, freeze fish filets in a small amount of water in a zip-seal bag—or have a local vendor vacuum-seal the filets for you and then freeze the package. Store the frozen fish in the bottom of your cheater pack.

IN CAMP

Prep time: 30 minutes / frying pan, foil, or Dutch oven

Keep the fish alive or chilled until the last minute before filleting and then marinating. Mix the dry herbs and spices with the mayonnaise and lime juice (or balsamic vinegar). Generously coat the filets with the sauce and let sit for 30 minutes before cooking. Wrap the filets in foil or arrange in a shallow pan and top with minced onion and lime slices. Cook on medium-low heat for about 20 minutes. If you are cooking in foil over coals or on a grill, double the layers of foil and shorten cooking time to 15 minutes. You won't have to turn this as the fish should poach in its own juices along with the jerk sauce.

Shopping List:	Number of Campers			
	2	4	6	12
Fresh Salmon, filets or steaks	1 lb	2 lbs	3 lbs	6 lbs
HERBS AND SPICES:				
Ground Oregano	pinch	¼ t	½ t	1 t
Thyme	pinch	¼ t	½ t	1 t
Black Pepper	pinch	¼ t	½ t	1 t
Ground Cayenne Pepper	¼ t	1/3 t	½ t	1 t
Ground Allspice	¼ t	1/3 t	½ t	1 t
Mayonnaise	¼ c	½ c	1 c	1½ c
Lime Juice or Balsamic Vinegar	1 t	2 t	3 t	2 T
Onion, diced				

VARIATIONS AND COMMENTS

You can use this recipe with any fish that is fairly fatty, like lake trout or fresh tuna. Whether you use fish or even chicken, this is a delicious dish despite its odd title. And, if you eat salmon often, it is a nice change. Take care to adjust the spiciness to taste—it can be very hot if you use a prepared sauce that uses a lot of Scotch Bonnet peppers. (If you can't find a prepared sauce, this version will come close.) Now the sauce isn't rocket science. Taste it first, it should have a pretty fair kick to it. Adjust to your taste. Remember, it won't be as spicy after it has cooked into the fish. Serve with a crunchy cabbage-based salad and slabs of garlic bread. If you are into presentations, this is a pretty dish.

F

I

S

H

FISH TAMPIQUEÑO

While guiding in the Bay Islands off Honduras, I needed to come up with many different ways to cook the fresh snapper and grouper that we bought from spear fishers in dugout canoes. This recipe was popular and created great leftovers for fish chowder.

AT HOME

If you are unable to acquire fresh fish during your trip, then at least 24 hours before your departure, freeze fish filets in a small amount of water in a zip-seal bag—or have a local vendor vacuum-seal the filets for you and then freeze the package. Store the frozen fish in the bottom of your cheater pack.

IN CAMP
Prep time: 30 minutes / one pot, frying pan, or foil

Keep the fish alive or chilled until the last minute before cooking. Sauté the veggies and garlic in olive oil for two minutes. Add cumin and chili powder and enough beer to make a centimeter-deep pool in the pan. Stir to mix. Nestle the filets into the beer and spoon the veggies over the fish. Place lime slices on top of the fish, cover the pan, and steam for 15 to 20 minutes—less if using thin filets. Serve with warm tortillas and Corn Cucumber Salad.

Shopping List:	Number of Campers			
	2	4	6	12
Fresh Fish, filets	1 lb	2 lbs	3 lbs	6 lbs
Onion, diced	½ c	1 c	1½ c	3 c
Bell Pepper, diced	½ c	1 c	1½ c	3 c
Jalapeño Peppers, fresh, seeded and diced	1	2	3	5
Garlic Cloves, minced	3	5	7	12
Beer (12 oz can)	6 oz	12 oz	12 oz	18 oz
Limes, for juice and garnish	1	2	3	5
HERBS AND SPICES:				
Cumin	1 t	1½ t	2 t	1 T
Chili Powder	½ t	¾ t	1 t	2 t

VARIATIONS AND COMMENTS

This is tasty served over a bed of rice. You can use any mild-tasting white fish for this. Yes, you can substitute salsa instead of making the sauce (Herdez Mexican Salsa Casera works well), but it will be a different flavor. Still good, but different. Both ways of cooking create excellent fare for fish tacos and burritos.

F

I

S

H

FISH IN TROPICAL-FRUIT GLAZE

While in Belize, I was stumped for another way to cook the fish that our local guides John and Elmo brought in—until I realized we had an abundance of overripe fruit ... hmmm, another idea is born.

AT HOME

If you are unable to acquire fresh fish during your trip, then at least 24 hours before your departure, freeze fish filets in a small amount of water in a zip-seal bag—or have a local vendor vacuum-seal the filets for you and then freeze the package. Store the frozen fish in the bottom of your cheater pack.

IN CAMP
Prep time: 30 minutes / two pans

Keep the fish alive or chilled until just before cooking. Filet to remove bones if whole. In a large pot, mash the banana. Add cantaloupe, pineapple and allspice and stir on low heat. On very low heat, add butter until just melted into the fruit. Remove from heat. In a shallow pan, arrange the filets with enough lime juice to cover the bottom. Spoon fruit sauce over the filets. Cover the pan and steam for 15 minutes or until the fish is flaky. Re-spoon the fruit sauce over the filets and serve with a rice dish and rum punch for a tropical treat!

Shopping List:	Number of Campers			
	2	4	6	12
Fresh Fish, filets	1 lb	2 lbs	3 lbs	6 lbs
Limes, for juice	2	3	4	6
Banana, ripe	1	1	2	3
Cantaloupe or similar melon, cubed	½ c	1 c	1½ c	2½ c
Pineapple, cubed	½ c	1 c	1½ c	2½ c
Butter (not oil)	1 T	1½ T	2½ T	4 T
HERBS AND SPICES:				
Allspice (or Cinnamon)	¼ t	½ t	¾ t	1½ t

VARIATIONS AND COMMENTS

This recipe works best with non-fishy tasting species like grouper and snapper. It is far and away my favorite way to prepare Yellowtail Snapper. The sauce is also good with a little grated coconut or walnuts mixed in. Although this recipe sounds odd, you will be delighted if you give it a try.

F

I

S

H

FISH TACOS OR BURRITOS

This dish may sound strange, but it is common to encounter such treats along coastal Mexico. Try it. Even non-fish eaters like this.

AT HOME

If you are unable to acquire fresh fish during your trip, then at least 24 hours before your departure, freeze fish filets in a small amount of water in a zip-seal bag—or have a local vendor vacuum-seal the filets for you and then freeze the package. Store the frozen fish in the bottom of your cheater pack.

Pan-fried trout with wild leeks.

F

I

S

H

IN CAMP
Prep time: 30 minutes / one pot, frying pan, or foil

Keep the fish alive or chilled until the last minute before cooking. Filet the fish if whole. Sauté half the onion and bell peppers, jalapeños, and garlic in olive oil for two minutes. Add cumin, lime juice, chili powder and enough beer to make a centimeter-deep pool in the pan. Stir to mix. Nestle the filets into the beer and spoon veggies over the fish. Cover the pan, and steam fish for 15 to 20 minutes—less if using thin filets.

After the fish is cooked and has cooled slightly (so you don't burn your fingers) flake the fish flesh into small pieces using a fork. Grate the cheese. Combine chopped Chinese cabbage with remaining half chopped onion and peppers with lime juice. Spoon fish into flour tortillas. Top with cheese and cabbage mixture to make burritos. If making tacos, simply spoon smaller amounts of the same goodies into soft corn tortillas that have been warmed in foil on the grill or in the pot with the fish.

Shopping List:	Number of Campers			
	2	4	6	12
Fresh Fish, filets	¾ lb	1½ lbs	2½ lbs	4 lbs
Onion (golf-ball size) diced and divided	1	2	3	5
Bell Pepper, diced and divided	1	1	2	4
Jalapeño Peppers, fresh, seeded and diced	1	2	3	5
Garlic Cloves, minced	1	2	3	5
Limes, for juice	1	2	3	5
Beer	6 oz	12 oz	12 oz	18 oz
Cheddar Cheese	4 oz	8 oz	12 oz	24 oz
Chinese Cabbage, chopped	1 c	1½ c	2 c	5 c
Flour Tortillas, 10" to 12" (for burritos)	4	8	12	24
OR				
Corn Rortillas, 6" (for tacos)	8	16	24	48
HERBS AND SPICES:				
Cumin	1 t	1½ t	2 t	1 T
Chili Powder	½ t	¾ t	1 t	2 t

VARIATIONS AND COMMENTS

I've made these tacos using grouper, snapper, pollack, rockfish, halibut, pike, John Dory (New Zealand fish), and shrimp—with great success. Let me know what interesting varieties you try.

F
I
S
H

137

GROUPER IN HORSERADISH DILL SAUCE

Working for Slickrock Adventures gave me many opportunities to dine on a great variety of recipes featuring Caribbean fish. One night, Cully Erdman put this gem together in the kitchen cabana. It is simple and fairly quick.

AT HOME

If you are unable to acquire fresh fish during your trip, then at least 24 hours before your departure, freeze fish filets in a small amount of water in a zip-seal bag—or have a local vendor vacuum-seal the filets for you and then freeze the package. Store the frozen fish in the bottom of your cheater pack.

IN CAMP

Prep time: 20 minutes / one pan or foil

Keep the fish alive or chilled until the last minute before cooking. Filet whole fish. Place filets in the bottom of a shallow pan with enough lime juice to cover the bottom. Spoon juice over the filets, then coat with horseradish sauce and sprinkle liberally with dill weed and black pepper. Cover and steam for 15 minutes without turning. Test for doneness by flaking with a fork. If flakes are no longer translucent it is ready.

Shopping List:	Number of Campers			
	2	**4**	**6**	**12**
Fresh fish, filets	1 lb	2 lbs	3 lbs	6 lbs
Limes, for juice	2	3	4	6
Horseradish Sauce (not pure horseradish)	2 oz	4 oz	6 oz	8 oz
HERBS AND SPICES:				
Dill	1 t	2 t	1 T	2 T
Black Pepper, to taste				

VARIATIONS AND COMMENTS

This recipe works best with salt-water species, including salmon, but different species of trout are good. The key is to have fairly thick filets. A little minced onion is a nice addition to the horseradish sauce. The leftovers make a great fish salad. It sure beats the heck out of a tuna-salad sandwich!

F

I

S

H

COCONUT GROUPER

This Caribbean favorite is crisp and crunchy on the outside and suc-culent on the inside. There are many island versions of this recipe; this is mine.

AT HOME

If you are unable to acquire fresh fish during your trip, then at least 24 hours before your departure, freeze fish filets in a small amount of water in a zip-seal bag—or have a local vendor vac-uum-seal the filets for you and then freeze the package. Store the frozen fish in the bottom of your cheater pack.

IN CAMP
Prep time: 40 minutes / two pans

Filet whole fish just before cooking. Roll filets in egg, then in bread crumbs, then in the egg again, and finally in the grated coconut. Put olive oil and butter in a pan on medium low heat. When the butter has melted, lay filets in the pan. When browned, turn once. Cook thick filets fairly slowly and cover while brown-ing. When done, both sides will be golden brown and it will look like a porcupine. Serve with a chopped pineapple and cabbage salad for a real feast.

Shopping List:	Number of Campers			
	2	**4**	**6**	**12**
Fresh Fish, filets	1 lb	2 lbs	3 lbs	6 lbs
Eggs, beaten	1	2	2	4
Olive Oil	1 T	2 T	3 T	5 T
Butter	1 T	2 T	3 T	5 T
Bread Crumbs (unseasoned)	2 T	3 T	½ c	1 c
Coconut, unsweetened, coarsely grated	¼ c	1c	1 ½ c	2½ c

HERBS AND SPICES:
Nada, it needs nothing.

VARIATIONS AND COMMENTS
This recipe works best with thick filets of grouper, but dolphin (mahimahi), snapper, and even walleye work well.

F
I
S
H

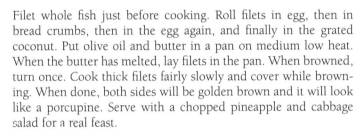

139

Foiled Again!

If you are a former scout, you probably recall meals in which various foil-wrapped mixtures of ground beef, carrots, and potatoes were thrown into a campfire and came out nearly weightless and inedible. Yeah, those were the days.

This section is loaded with meals that are perfect for the first or second night of a paddle trip, wonderful for camping with a car, or even the first night of a weekend backpacking excursion.

The packets are prepared at home well in advance of your trip and frozen. You can even mix or match to build a multi-course meal worthy of a backcountry dinner party. Smaller meals can be cooked in camp on a griddle, but these are best when cooked on hot coals. (Charcoal in a fire pan works perfectly well, as does tossing these in your Woody.)

Before you plan a meal that requires an open fire, check the rules for where you will be going. Many national parks do not allow open fires in backcountry sites, and there are occasional fire bans during dry periods in most areas.

One word of caution: If you make your packets too far ahead of time, they will get eaten at home before you depart—for the same reasons you will love them in camp. If you can't resist, pop them in a 400° F oven and, voilà, you have a great home-cooked meal.

CARIBBEAN CARROTS

This a good use for those pseudo-baby carrots that seem to be ever-present in the veggie drawer.

AT HOME

Wash carrots. Drain off excess water and put carrots in a mixing bowl. Add all of the ingredients and toss until carrots are well coated. Dump the carrots on one half of a double layer of long sheets of aluminum foil (shiny side in). Fold over and seal with three tight folds.

IN CAMP

Prep time: 20 minutes / No pans!

You need a fire. If you are traveling in an area where it is okay to have one, build a wood fire and let it establish a good bed of hot coals. Draw some coals off to one side of the flame with a stick and lay the foil packet on the hot coals for 10 minutes per side. An alternative is to bring charcoal briquettes in a paper bag that you can lay on a twig fire. This will give you a bed of hot coals in no time.

Shopping List:	Number of Campers			
	2	4	6	12
Baby Carrots	8 oz	1 lb	1½ lbs	3 lbs
Olive Oil	2 t	1 T	1½ T	3 T
HERBS AND SPICES:				
Maple Syrup	1 T	2 T	2 T	1/3 c
Jerk Seasoning, powdered	1 t	2 t	1 T	2 T
Black Pepper, to taste				

VARIATIONS AND COMMENTS

Use sliced sweet potatoes instead of carrots. Omit the syrup (the potatoes will be sweet enough) and reduce the cooking time by 5 minutes. Or use a Cajun spice instead of jerk seasoning. Realize these are both hot, savory spice mixtures, so adjust to taste.

F
O
I
L
E
D

PESTO-ROASTED SPUDS

These smell so good when they are sizzlin' on the fire, you won't have to call anyone to tell them chow's ready. Expect a Pavlovian response.

AT HOME

Rinse and cut up red potatoes into quarters. Keep the skins on. Put the potatoes in a bowl and add the pesto. Stir well to coat potatoes uniformly in this fragrant basil mixture. Stir in grated Parmesan cheese. Dump the potatoes onto one half of a double layer of long sheets of aluminum foil (shiny side in). Fold over and seal with three tight folds.

IN CAMP

Prep time: 30 minutes / No pans!

You need a fire. If you are traveling in an area where it is okay to have one, build a wood fire and let it establish a good bed of hot coals. Draw some coals off to one side of the flame with a stick and lay the foil packet on the hot coals for 15 minutes per side. An alternative is to bring charcoal briquettes in a paper bag that you can lay on a twig fire. This will give you a bed of hot coals in no time.

Shopping List:	Number of Campers			
	2	**4**	**6**	**12**
Red Potatoes	1 lb	2 lbs	3 lbs	6 lbs
Parmesan Cheese, grated	2 oz	4 oz	4 oz	8 oz
HERBS AND SPICES:				
Pesto, make it yourself or buy it	2 oz	4 oz	4 oz	8 oz
Black Pepper, to taste				

VARIATIONS AND COMMENTS

Toss in some chopped onion with the potatoes or use roasted red pepper pesto—dynamite!

F
O
I
L
E
D

SALMON POACHED IN FRESH HERB SAUCE

Lots of people are eating salmon these days with an eye toward a healthier diet. They are also discovering that there are many ways to cook salmon. This is an easy and tasty choice.

AT HOME
Rinse salmon filets and cut them into 8-ounce chunks. Score the skin side of each chunk with four shallow cuts. Mix the sauce ingredients in a bowl, toss in the salmon, and stir a bit. Crease a doubled sheet of foil so you have two halves. Fold the edges up on one half to create a dam to hold the juice. Dump the fish and wine mixture on the foil, fold over the other half and seal it with three or four tight folds. Freeze solid.

IN CAMP
Prep time: 15 minutes / No pans!

You need a fire. If you are traveling in an area where it is appropriate to have one, build a wood fire and let it establish a good bed of hot coals. Draw some coals off to one side of the flame with a stick and lay the foil packet on the hot coals for about 8 minutes per side. (The foil should puff up slightly when cooked if it has been sealed well.) An alternative is to bring charcoal briquettes in a paper bag that you can lay on a twig fire. This will give you a bed of hot coals in no time. This is really great with Garlic Smashed Spuds and a Greek Cabbage Salad.

Shopping List:	Number of Campers			
	2	**4**	**6**	**12**
Salmon, filets	1 lb	2 lbs	3 lbs	6 lbs
Red Onion, diced	½ c	1 c	1½ c	3 c
Sour Cream	½ c	1 c	1 c	2½ c
White Wine	½ c	1c	1½ c	2½ c
HERBS AND SPICES:				
Garlic Cloves, minced	2	4	6	12
Fresh Basil or Rosemary, chopped	1 oz	2 oz	3 oz	4oz
Black Pepper, to taste				

VARIATIONS AND COMMENTS
You can use just about any fresh herb, except sage. The sour cream can be omitted if you like, but it picks up beautiful flavors from the wine and herbs and makes a rich sauce that goes great with potatoes or spooned over rice. Bear in mind that freezing will split the cream, so the sauce will seem curdled. Don't let that bother you, it will still taste wonderful. You will definitely want to eat this at home.

F
O
I
L
E
D

BACON-WRAPPED ONIONS

Easy to make and a delicious mate to any of the other foil entrees.

AT HOME

Peel one tennis-ball sized onion per person. With a paring knife, cut out the center of each onion, like you would core an apple. Stuff two peeled cloves of garlic into the middle of each onion and tightly wrap two strips of raw bacon around each onion. Place each onion on a double square of foil, sprinkle with water, salt, pepper, and rosemary. Sealing each onion tightly by itself holds all of the goods together. This is best if made fresh before a trip rather than frozen.

IN CAMP
Prep time: 25 minutes / No pans!

You need a fire. If you are traveling in an area where it is appropriate to have one, build a wood fire and let it establish a good bed of hot coals. Draw some coals off to one side of the flame with a stick and lay the foil packet on the hot coals for 10 minutes per side. An alternative is to bring charcoal briquettes in a paper bag that you can lay on a twig fire. This will give you a bed of hot coals in no time. The onions smell terrific when cooking and the bacon will keep them well oiled so they won't stick to the foil.

Shopping List:	Number of Campers			
	2	4	6	12
Onions	2	4	6	12
Garlic Cloves	2	4	6	12
Bacon Strips	4	8	12	24

HERBS AND SPICES:
Rosemary (or Thyme)
Black Pepper

F
O
I
L
E
D

VARIATIONS AND COMMENTS

Feel free to try any herb on this one. I think stuffing the onions with pepperoni might be delicious, too. A mixture of sun-dried tomatoes, garlic, and chopped red sweet pepper in olive oil are also a good bet. If you use a less oily meat or omit the meat entirely, be sure to coat the onions in olive oil, otherwise all those wonderful sugars in the onion will cause them to burn and the foil to stick.

CHEESY HAM AND SPUD BAKE

If this isn't comfort food, then nothing is. This is a real rib-sticker after a big energy day.

AT HOME
Wash and thinly slice the potatoes. You can use any variety—and leave the skins on if you like. Spread out a double layer of foil and drizzle a bit of olive oil over all of it. Layer the sliced potatoes, shredded cheddar, a few onions, and the sliced ham on half of the foil. Repeat. Sprinkle liberally with fresh ground pepper. Fold the empty half of the oiled foil over and seal tightly. Freeze.

IN CAMP
Prep time: 40 minutes / No pans!

You need a fire. If you are traveling in an area where it is appropriate to have one, build a wood fire and let it establish a good bed of hot coals. Draw some coals off to one side of the flame with a stick and lay the foil packet on the hot coals for 20 to 25 minutes per side. An alternative is to bring charcoal briquettes in a paper bag that you can lay on a twig fire. This will give you a bed of hot coals in no time. The Bacon-Wrapped Onions go great with this.

Shopping List:	Number of Campers			
	2	4	6	12
Ham, deli-style, sliced	4 oz	8 oz	12 oz	1½ lbs
Potatoes, sliced	I lb	2 lbs	3 lbs	6 lbs
Onion, diced	½ c	1 c	1½ c	3 c
Cheddar Cheese, shredded	½ c	1 c	1½ c	3 c

HERBS AND SPICES:
Black Pepper, to taste

VARIATIONS AND COMMENTS
Add sliced sweet potatoes or carrots into the mix. A few herbs tossed in with the black pepper will contribute a more complex flavor.

F
O
I
L
E
D

MESQUITE-ROASTED CHICKEN BREAST

This is a tasty meal.

AT HOME

Rinse skinless and boneless chicken breasts. Cut into halves. In a bowl mix the onion, garlic, BBQ sauce (Mesquite-flavored or whatever you prefer), and the pepper. Add the chicken and coat well with the sauce. Tear two sheets of foil (shiny side in) the size of a legal pad. Pour the chicken mixture onto the double layer of foil, fold in half, and seal the edges with three tight folds. For easy and quick cooking and packing ease, divide into 2-person pouches.

IN CAMP
Prep time: 20 minutes / No pans!

You need a fire. If you are traveling in an area where it is appropriate to have one, build a wood fire and let it establish a good bed of hot coals. Draw some coals off to one side of the flame with a stick and lay the foil packet on the hot coals for 10 minutes per side. An alternative is to bring charcoal briquettes in a paper bag that you can lay on a twig fire. This will give you a bed of hot coals in no time. Serve with a couple foil veggie sides, like Pesto-Roasted Spuds and Caribbean Carrots.

Shopping List:	Number of Campers			
	2	**4**	**6**	**12**
Chicken Breast, boneless	1 lb	2 lbs	3 lbs	6 lbs
Sweet Onion, diced	½ c	1 c	1½ c	3 c
HERBS AND SPICES:				
Garlic Cloves, minced	2	4	6	12
BBQ Sauce	½ c	1 c	1½ c	2½ c
Black Pepper, to taste				

F
O
I
L
E
D

VARIATIONS AND COMMENTS

Sprinkle a handful of fresh chopped chives onto the chicken before sealing the foil. Virtually any sauce or marinade will work, including Italian dressing. Try this recipe at home when you want a good meal but only have time to pop something in the oven. Forty minutes at 350 degrees and you're done.

WILD MUSHROOM CHICKEN MARSALA

Get out the candles! This meal is worthy of a backcountry celebration.

AT HOME

Rinse skinless and boneless chicken breasts. Cut into thin slices, discarding any fat or skin. In a bowl, whisk the cornstarch into the wine and then add all other ingredients. Mix well. Add the chicken strips, and mix again. Take a large sheet of foil and double it. Crease it so you have two halves. Fold the edges up on one half to create a dam to hold in the juice. Dump the chicken and marinade on the foil. Seal the foil with three or four tight folds. Chill overnight for the mushrooms to rehydrate or freeze before you travel. For easy and quick cooking and packing ease, divide into 2-person pouches.

IN CAMP
Prep time: 20 minutes / No pans!

You need a fire. If you are traveling in an area where it is appropriate to have one, build a wood fire and let it establish a good bed of hot coals. Draw some coals off to one side of the flame with a stick and lay the foil packet on the hot coals for 10 minutes per side. An alternative is to bring charcoal briquettes in a paper bag that you can lay on a twig fire. This will give you a bed of hot coals in no time. The foil pouch will puff up as it cooks. Cut a hole in the top and spoon chicken and the incredible sauce over penne pasta or Garlic Smashed Spuds. A nice Pinot Grigio wouldn't hurt either.

Shopping List:	Number of Campers			
	2	4	6	12
Chicken Breast, boneless	1 lb	2 lbs	3 lbs	6 lbs
Marsala, Madeira or Sweet Vermouth Wine	1 c	1½ c	2 c	4 c
Cornstarch	½ t	1 t	1½ t	1 T
Dried Mushrooms (porcini or shitake)	1 oz	2 oz	3 oz	5 oz
Onion, diced	½ c	1 c	1½ c	3 c
HERBS AND SPICES:				
Garlic Cloves, minced	2	4	6	12
Fresh Rosemary sprigs	1	2	3	6
Black Pepper, to taste				

F
O
I
L
E
D

VARIATIONS AND COMMENTS

Try fresh marjoram instead of the rosemary and/or substitute fresh white button mushrooms for the dry ones. They will freeze fine. If you really want to go for the gold, use dried morel mushrooms. You'll soon be the camp deity.

PIZZA CHICKEN

Here's a meal everyone seems to like—especially kids.

AT HOME

Rinse boneless and skinless chicken breasts. Cut each breast in half and then cut a deep slit sideways into each half. Rub a little spaghetti or pizza sauce inside the slits and then stuff with chopped mushroom, garlic, and sliced provolone cheese. Take a large double sheet of foil, score in half and drizzle sauce on it. Lay the stuffed chicken breasts in the pool of sauce, pour on more sauce, seal tightly, and freeze. For easy and quick cooking and packing ease, divide into 2-person pouches.

IN CAMP
Prep time: 20 minutes / one pot

You need a fire. If you are traveling in an area where it is appropriate to have one, build a wood fire and let it establish a good bed of hot coals. Draw some coals off to one side of the flame with a stick and lay the foil packet on the hot coals for 10 minutes per side. An alternative is to bring charcoal briquettes in a paper bag that you can lay on a twig fire. This will give you a bed of hot coals in no time. While the chicken is cooking, boil some pasta. Serve the hot chicken and red sauce over the pasta. Sprinkle Italian cheese on top. I love Asiago cheese on this. It has just the right balance between mild and sharp.

Shopping List:	Number of Campers			
	2	4	6	12
Chicken Breast, boneless	1 lb	2 lbs	3 lbs	6 lbs
Pizza or Spaghetti sauce	8 oz	16 oz	24 oz	48 oz
Fresh Mushrooms, chopped	¼ c	½ c	1 c	2 c
Provolone or Mozzarella Cheese, shredded	4 oz	6 oz	8 oz	1 lb
HERBS AND SPICES:				
Garlic Cloves, minced	2	4	6	12
Black Pepper, to taste				

F

O

I

L

E

D

VARIATIONS AND COMMENTS

Try stuffing the chicken with pepperoni instead of mushrooms or add chopped onion and spinach to the mushroom mixture for a Florentine twist. Oh, more sauce is always better and can be added at the end over the hot pasta.

Chapter 12

DESSERTS

Dessert as a Safety Precaution

During a mid-1980's kayak tour in Resurrection Bay, Alaska, we found dessert to be essential safety equipment. As nighttime temperatures plunged into the forties, one of our guests was often too chilled to sleep well, which also meant that her partner didn't sleep either. Too many nights like that in a row not only compromise a vacation, but people's well-being on a wilderness trip. We had tried a number of clothing options to improve her sleeping comfort but all proved inadequate.

In the end, the answer was ... instant cheesecake. On night four, we whipped up a rich dessert as an ending to a particularly nice paddling day. All those fats and sugars had our companion sleeping like a baby. Consequently, her husband also enjoyed a good night's sleep. Fats and sugars are simply calories—and calories are a measurement of heat.

So, don't be afraid to stoke that furnace before you turn in on a chilly evening.

BAKED APPLE DUMPLINGS

This works in the oven at home, too. It begs to be served with vanilla ice cream or camp whipped cream.

AT HOME

Wash and core one small apple per person. Mix the other ingredients in a bowl. Cut a square of previously frozen or homemade pie pastry and lay it on a large doubled and oiled square of foil that is larger than the pastry square. Place one apple in the middle of the pastry and fill the hole with the sugar mixture. Put a dab of butter on top of the filling and fold the pastry up and over the whole apple. Do the same with the foil. Seal tightly. Freeze until ready to travel.

IN CAMP
Prep time: 40 minutes / No pans!

You need a fire. If you are traveling in an area where it is appropriate to have one, build a wood fire and let it establish a good bed of hot coals. Draw some coals off to one side of the flame with a stick and spread the foil-covered apples over them so they are not touching. Keep turning the apples regularly so they don't sit on the coals for more than 6 to 8 minutes in one spot. This is labor intensive, but the result is a truly outstanding dessert. Don't try this in bear country, as it will call critters ten miles away with the sweet aroma it produces.

Shopping List:	Number of Campers			
	2	**4**	**6**	**12**
Apples, small	2	4	6	12
Brown Sugar	¼ c	½ c	¾ c	1½ c
Walnuts, chopped	¼ c	½ c	¾ c	1½ c
Butter	1 T	2 T	3 T	6 T
Pastry dough, homemade or frozen	1 crust	2 crusts	3 crusts	6 crusts
SPICES:				
Cinnamon	½ t	1 t	1½ t	1 T
Nutmeg	¼ t	½ t	¾ t	1½ t

D E S S E R T S

VARIATIONS AND COMMENTS

Drizzling a little rum or brandy into the sugar mixture doesn't hurt a thing! You can also make these without the pastry portion, just reduce the cooking time by 8-10 minutes.

GEORGIA PEACH CAKE

This is basically foolproof. Even if you are sort of … well … let's say "cooking challenged," you will pull off this recipe with style to spare!

AT HOME

Package a yellow cake mix into a zip-seal bag (a half-gallon size is ideal if you can find them) that can act as a mixing bowl, along with egg powder if you aren't planning to use fresh eggs. Remember to bring the directions from the mix box.

IN CAMP
Prep time: 45 minutes / one baking pan

Open a can of peaches. With a knife, chop the peaches in small pieces while still in the can. Add chopped peaches and juice to the bag of dry cake mix, along with a small amount of canola oil and fresh eggs if you are using them. Omit water that the mix calls for. The peach syrup replaces it. Seal and fondle until you have a well-mixed batter.

Preheat an oiled baking pan with a tight-fitting lid on a medium flame. Squeeze the batter into the pan. Cover tightly and insulate cover with a dry towel. Reduce heat to lowest flame and be sure the stove is in a wind-sheltered spot. I use a heat diffuser plate and rotate the pan one quarter turn every 10 minutes. Resist the temptation to lift the lid until it has been baking about 30 minutes. The cake is done when the center feels fairly firm or a pine needle comes out fairly clean.

Shopping List:

Number of Campers
Makes enough for 10, but the leftovers keep well!

Yellow Cake Mix (use whatever brand you prefer)
Peaches in light syrup, 15 oz can
Eggs, according to mix
Oil, according to mix

VARIATIONS AND COMMENTS:
This also works great with canned pineapple, apricots, or cherries. You can even use blueberries for a blueberry muffin cake! Excellent with vanilla cream or camp whipped cream.

D
E
S
S
E
R
T
S

ONE-BURNER BROWNIES

There is nothing like a hot fudgy brownie on a cool evening after a day of challenging weather.

AT HOME

Re-package brownie mix in a zip-seal bag (quart size freezer bag is ideal) that can double as a mixing bowl. Add egg powder if you aren't planning to use fresh eggs. Remember to bring the directions from the mix box.

IN CAMP

Prep time: 45 minutes / one baking pan or Woody

Follow directions on the mix. Add liquid ingredients to the zip-seal bag with the dry ingredients. Seal and fondle the mixture until a consistent batter is achieved. You can use half the amount of oil called for—or omit it all together. It still seems to work just fine. The oil helps keep the brownies moist if there are any leftovers—but that doesn't seem to happen.

Preheat an oiled baking pan with a tight-fitting lid on a medium flame. Squeeze batter into the pan and spread uniformly with a spoon. Add any additional flavorings (see variations section that follows) at this time. Cover tightly and insulate the cover with a dry camp towel. Reduce heat to lowest flame and be sure the stove is in a wind-sheltered spot. I use an aluminum windscreen and heat diffuser plate to help avoid burning. You should also rotate the pan a quarter-turn every 10 minutes. Brownies will take about 40 minutes to bake. The top will appear sticky, but take them off and let them cool for 30 minutes before cutting and serving.

D
E
S
S
E
R
T
S

Shopping List:
Brownie Mix that makes up to 12 servings
Water, according to mix
Oil, according to mix
Egg or Egg Substitute, according to mix

VARIATIONS FOR BROWNIES

There is certainly nothing wrong with a chewy batch of plain chocolate brownies—but why stop there? Brownies are forgiving to make and have infinite possibilities. Try some of these:

- Instead of water, use rum or brandy for the liquid.

- **Linzer Brownies**: simply swirl a half cup of raspberry jam into the batter before you bake it.

- **Black Forest Brownies**: soak a handful of dried cherries in warm rum for an hour before preparing the brownie mix. Use the same amount of rum as the water the mix calls for. Add the re-hydrated cherries to the dry mix. These are amazing. Definitely try this at home.

- **Bailey's Brownies:** Add a shot of Irish Crème to the liquid components added to the dry brownie mix. These smell heavenly as they bake.

- **Tropical Brownies:** Simply slice a couple bananas into the batter before baking. They are even better if the bananas have been somewhat abused. Banana chips work too if you first soak them in warm water for 10 minutes. These sound funky, but they are really great.

- **Are You Nuts?** I like nuts in my brownies, so I try something different now and then, like pecan halves or whole almonds that have been toasted for a few minutes in the baking pan prior to adding the batter.

- **Reese's Brownies:** Drop about a half cup of peanut butter by the teaspoonful throughout brownie batter after it is in the pan. Run a knife back and forth to swirl the peanut butter through the batter.

- **Cream Cheese Brownies:** Drop about four ounces of softened cream cheese by the teaspoonful throughout the batter after it is in the pan. Run a knife back and forth to swirl the cheese through the batter.

D
E
S
S
E
R
T
S

EASY BLACK FOREST CAKE

This is another easy recipe with amazing aromas, sure to be eaten with a spoon as it usually turns out on the moist and gooey side.

AT HOME

Package a dark-chocolate cake mix into a zip-seal bag (a half-gallon size bag is ideal) that can double as a mixing bowl, along with egg powder if you aren't planning to use fresh eggs. Remember to bring the directions from the mix box.

IN CAMP
Prep time: 45 minutes / one baking pan

Open the can of cherry pie filling; reserve half of the liquid for a topping. Add the remainder of the filling to the bag of dry cake mix. Add fresh eggs if you have not used egg powder, a small amount of canola oil, and water. Seal the bag and fondle until you have a well-mixed batter. Pre-heat oiled baking pan with a tight-fitting lid on medium flame. Squeeze the batter into the baking pan. Cover tightly and insulate the cover with a dry towel. Reduce heat to lowest flame and be sure the stove is in a wind-sheltered spot. I use a heat diffuser plate and rotate the pan one quarter turn every 10 minutes. Resist the temptation to lift the lid until it has been baking about 30 minutes. The cake is done when the center feels fairly firm or a pine needle comes out fairly clean.

Shopping List:

Number of Campers
Makes enough for 10, but the leftovers keep well!

Dark-Chocolate Cake Mix (use whatever brand you prefer)
2-3 Eggs, according to mix
Oil, according to mix
Water, according to mix
Cherry Pie filling, 15 oz can

VARIATIONS AND COMMENTS
You can use re-hydrated dried cherries, or fresh blueberries or raspberries. Excellent with vanilla cream or camp whipped cream.

D
E
S
S
E
R
T
S

 154

ALASKAN PANCAKE LAYER CAKE

This is an easy way to make a special dessert for a celebration. It was an impromptu invention near the base of Denali when I discovered someone in our group was having a birthday. It turned into an 8 layer birthday cake.

AT HOME
Package a Devil's Food cake mix into a zip-seal bag (a half-gallon size is ideal if you can find them) that can act as a mixing bowl, along with egg powder if you aren't planning to use fresh eggs. Remember to bring the directions from the mix box.

IN CAMP
Prep time: 30 minutes / one frying pan

Add a little less water than the instructions call for and a bit more canola oil, and fresh eggs if you are using them, to the bag of dry cake mix. Seal and fondle until you have a mixture the consistency of thick pancake batter.

Preheat a small amount of oil in an 8- to 10-inch frying pan on a medium flame. When the pan is medium-hot, pour in enough batter to make an 8-inch pancake. Cook as you would a breakfast pancake by carefully flipping when the edges look done. Repeat until you have six to eight pancakes of similar size stacked on a plate. Liberally spread each cake with a layer of red raspberry or blackberry jam. Stack them together. Press down on them to glue together, sprinkle the top layer with powdered sugar, and slice as you would a layered cake.

Shopping List:	Number of Campers
	Serves up to 8

Devils Food Cake Mix (use whatever brand you prefer)
Raspberry or Blackberry Jam, 8 to 12 oz

EXTRA CREDIT VERSION:
Drizzle Irish Crème over each serving.
Powdered Sugar

D
E
S
S
E
R
T
S

VARIATIONS AND COMMENTS
I highly recommend making this dessert to mark a special event for a chocolate lover—especially if you need points. For a non-chocolate version, try spice cake mix with apple butter spread between the layers. This is also good with vanilla cream or simple cream-cheese icing.

BACKCOUNTRY PEACH COBBLER

This takes a bit of effort but is truly a comforting sweet on a chilly evening.

AT HOME

Re-package dry baking mix ingredients into a quart-sized zip-seal bag. Bisquick or Jiffy baking mixes work fine. However, if you can find minimally packaged buttermilk biscuit mixes, use those. They work even better. Remember to bring the directions from the mix.

IN CAMP

Prep time: 50 minutes / one baking pan

For trips where weight isn't a big deal, I use canned peaches heavily laced with cinnamon. Do not drain the syrup as it will soak into the biscuits as they bake. For weight-conscious trips, use dried peaches that you re-hydrate in enough hot water to cover them for one hour before baking. Add a half cup of brown sugar and one teaspoon of cinnamon to the peaches and hot water to form tasty syrup.

To make the dough: Gradually add water (follow directions from the mix) to the dry ingredients in the bag. Reseal and fondle until you get a thick batter that is the consistency of oatmeal. Relax. It really doesn't matter if it is too thick or too thin.

Preheat an oiled baking pan with a tight-fitting lid on medium flame. Spread all of the peach mixture into the hot pan. Squeeze the biscuit batter in lumps over the fruit. Sprinkle with brown sugar. Cover tightly and insulate the cover with a dry towel. Reduce heat to lowest flame and be sure your stove is in a wind-sheltered spot. I use a heat diffuser plate to avoid burning. You can also rotate the pan a quarter turn every 10 minutes. Cobbler is ready in 50 minutes.

Shopping List:	Number of Campers			
	4	6	8	12
Baking Mix				
(Bisquick, Jiffy, or Buttermilk)	1½ c	2½ c	4 c	5 c
Peaches, canned	15 oz	15 oz	24 oz	39 oz
Or Peaches, dried	1 c	1½ c	2 c	2½ c
SPICES:				
Cinnamon	1½ t	2 t	1 T	1½ T
Brown Sugar	1 T	1½ T	2 T	3 T

VARIATIONS AND COMMENTS

If you are going for camp guru status you can pack some whipping cream in your cheater pack and either whip it by shaking vigorously in a large Nalgene bottle or simply lace it with vanilla extract or Irish Crème and pour over steaming cobbler in camper's cups. Shake hard and fast and stop just as it thickens a bit. If you overdo it, you'll make butter!

BLACKBERRY PEACH COBBLER

For those of you who live in the Pacific Northwest and find yourself entangled in lovely blackberries each fall, try this for a treat.

Use the ingredients and directions for Backcountry Peach Cobbler. The only change is to add freshly foraged blackberries to the peach syrup, per the following guidelines:

Shopping List:	Number of Campers			
	4	6	8	12
Blackberries	1 c	1½ c	2 c	3 c

VARIATIONS AND COMMENTS

Try other wild berries, like blueberries or raspberries. Blueberry peach cobbler is amazing with vanilla cream!

APPLE CRUMBLE

This is a simple dessert that uses dry lightweight ingredients. And I've yet to meet anyone who doesn't enjoy this.

AT HOME

Package the dry mix ingredients in one zip-seal plastic bag. In a separate zip-seal bag package the dried apples and spices.

IN CAMP

Prep time: 40 minutes / one baking pan

In a baking pan, simmer the spiced dried apples in enough water to cover them. Cover the pan and cook on medium flame until the apples re-hydrate. Add a bit more water and sugar to create syrup. Cut butter into the dry crumble mix with a fork and blend with just enough water to get it to barely stick together. Next, spoon this mixture over the apples, cover, and bake for 15 to 20 minutes.

Shopping List:	Number of Campers			
	4	6	8	12
Dried Apples	4 oz	6 oz	8 oz	12 oz
CRUMBLE INGREDIENTS*:				
Rolled Oats (not instant)	1 c	1½ c	2 c	2½ c
Biscuit Mix (like Bisquick)	½ c	¾ c	1 c	1½ c
Brown Sugar	½ c	¾ c	1 c	1½ c
Walnuts, chopped	½ c	¾ c	1 c	1½ c
Butter	1 T	1 T	2 T	¼ c
SPICES:				
Cinnamon	1½ t	2 t	1 T	1½ T
Nutmeg	1 t	1 t	1½ t	2 t
Brown Sugar (for apples)	1 T	1½ T	2 T	3 T
*Granola or Muesli (instead of making the crumble mix)	2 c	3 c	4 c	5 c

D
E
S
S
E
R
T
S

VARIATIONS AND COMMENTS

If you live in a city that has a Middle Eastern grocery you may be able to find a dessert cream in a tetrapack container that is preserved by ultra-high temperature (UHT). This is a nice substitute for whipped cream and is delicious on Apple Crumble. *Easy alternative is using granola or muesli.

BANANAS NIGEL FOSTER

This fun and fast dessert is inspired by paddling legend Nigel Foster.

AT HOME
Choose green bananas to travel better. They sweeten as they are cooked.

IN CAMP
Prep time: 15 minutes / one pan

Peel bananas and split in half lengthwise. Heat a small amount of butter in a frying pan on medium heat. Brown the bananas on their round sides in the butter. Turn and begin to brown on the flat side. Sprinkle with a handful of brown sugar, add rum (not a good time to hover over the pan), and flame the evaporating alcohol with your stove. Stir while the sugars caramelize. Serve each person two halves of a banana, flat side up, sprinkled with a few dark-chocolate chips and covered with a spoonful of the rum caramel sauce from the pan.

Shopping List:	Number of Campers			
	2	**4**	**6**	**12**
Bananas	2	4	6	12
Rum or Brandy	1 T	2 T	3 T	2/3 c
Butter	1 T	2 T	3 T	½ c
Brown Sugar	1 T	2 T	3 T	½ c
Chocolate Chips (the darker the better)	¼ c	½ c	¾ c	1½ c

VARIATIONS AND COMMENTS
For extra credit, top with dessert cream. Substitute brandy for rum or partially re-hydrated dried tropical fruit for the chocolate chips.

D
E
S
S
E
R
T
S

HOT APPLESAUCE

By using dried apples you can make this a dish light enough to carry in your backpack. I have used this recipe for the last 25 years and people always love it.

AT HOME

Package the dried apples with cinnamon and brown sugar in a zip-seal plastic bag.

IN CAMP

Prep time: 15 to 20 minutes / one pot

Cover dried apples with a half inch of water in a pot. Bring to a boil, reduce flame, and cover. Simmer until apples break down when stirred. Add additional cinnamon, brown sugar, and a pinch of nutmeg if you like. The brown sugar brings out the homemade applesauce flavor.

Shopping List:	Number of Campers			
	2	4	6	12
Dried apples	½ c	1 c	1½ c	3 c
SPICES:				
Cinnamon	½ t	1 t	2 t	1 T
Nutmeg	pinch	¼ t	½ t	1 t
Brown Sugar	1 t	2 t	1 T	2 T

D
E
S
S
E
R
T
S

VARIATIONS AND COMMENTS

Sprinkle with granola. You can also make this using other fruits like dried cherries or peaches, for a hot fruit compote.

DESSERT CREAMS AND TOPPINGS

Toppings can range from a can of whipped cream stored in your cheater pack to camp-made products. I routinely use the following—but you may come up with some good concoctions of your own ... let me know.

WHIPPED CREAM VARIATIONS

- Ultra-pasteurized whipping cream travels well in a soft-sided cooler and will last a day longer than your ice. Simply pour the cream into a clean liter-sized water bottle and shake vigorously until it starts to thicken. Add a half teaspoon of vanilla extract and a pinch of powdered sugar. Shake to blend. Don't try to shake the bottle until you get really thick cream or you will end up with butter instead.

- Some ethnic markets sell Ultra High Temperature preserved creams and canned dessert creams. These can be flavored with vanilla extract or a liqueur, like Irish Crème or Amaretto, to make a tasty topping.

- Pour a small can of evaporated milk in a clean water bottle. Add a little cold water, a pinch of sugar, and some vanilla extract. Shake the heck out of it and you end up with a foamy tasty topping for hot chocolate, coffee, or cake!

SIMPLE CREAM-CHEESE ICING

Soften eight ounces of cream cheese (Neufchatel works, too). In a bowl mix the cream cheese with two tablespoons of powdered sugar, a few ounces of water or milk, and a teaspoon of vanilla extract. This makes a fine icing for all sorts of goodies. Add two tablespoons of cocoa powder and two more of powdered sugar for chocolate icing.

Extra Credit: Add a tablespoon of Irish crème in place of milk or water.

D
E
S
S
E
R
T
S

BACKWORD

Dear Gentle Reader,

Having been on a few long adventures in my sordid past there are a couple of things you recognize early on: who you go with is more important than where you go; food is a lot more than just sustenance; making and eating food is a social event; some days it is THE event of the day.

Eating well in the field is an art that takes years to learn. Michael Gray has put together this book that will save you years of time figuring out what you can take, how to take it, how much you need for different size groups, and how to prepare it.

Getting this info from Michael is like getting a private guitar lesson from Eric Clapton!

Your pal,

Russell (Farrow)

Appendix A

Sample Meal Plans

WEEKEND TRIP WITH KIDS
Car Camping with Foil and Fire. No pans to clean!

BREAKFASTS:

Day 1:   Pumpkin Pancakes (page 59). For style points, bring along a can of whipped cream.

Day 2:   Jamie's Eggs Durango (page 48)

Day 3:   Kathleen's Cherry-Nut Crunch Granola (page 46)

LUNCHES AND SNACKS:

Trail Mix (½ M & M's, ¼ almonds, ¼ dried cherries)

Bagels, peanut butter, raspberry jelly, cream cheese, cheddar crackers, carrots, and apples

DINNERS:

Day 1:   Cheesy Ham and Spud Bake (page 145)

Day 2:   Pizza Chicken, for the kids (page 148)

Wild Mushroom Chicken Marsala, for the adults (page 147)

Day 3:   Pesto-Roasted Spuds (page 142)
Salmon Poached in Fresh Herb Sauce (page 143)

DESSERTS:

Baked Apple Dumplings (page 150)

Don't forget the s'mores. Try using dark-chocolate frosting instead of the traditional Hershey's candy bar. The frosting won't fall off the graham cracker.

LIGHTWEIGHT FOUR-DAY
BACKPACKING OR HIKING TRIP

BREAKFASTS:

Day 1:   Simple 10-minute, 3-Course Breakfast (page 44)

Days 2 & 4:   Kiwi Muesli (page 45)

Day 3:   Huevos Rancheros—use egg powder (page 47)

LUNCHES AND SNACKS:

Day 1:   Hummus With Pita and Veggies (page 67)

Day 2, 3 & 4:   Crackers, cheese, tortillas, pouched chicken or tuna,
                small packets of salad dressing (to make chicken or
                tuna salad), dried fruit, and bits of chocolate

DINNERS:

Day 1:   Easy Quesadillas, with pouched chicken added
                (page 68)

Day 2:   Meaty Vegetarian Chili (page 112). Use leftovers
                for Day 3 breakfast.

Day 3:   One-Pot Fried Rice—use egg powder and dried
                veggies (page 101)

Day 4:   Couscous Medley (page 98)

DESSERTS:

Instant chocolate pudding topped with Kathleen's Cherry-Nut Granola

FOUR-DAY TRIP (KAYAK/CANOE/BASE CAMP)

BREAKFASTS:

Days 1 & 4:   Kathleen's Cherry-Nut Granola (page 46)

Day 2:   Breakfast Tacos (page 50)

Day 3:   Rudy's Island Pancakes (page 57)

LUNCHES AND SNACKS:

Day 1:   Hummus With Pita and Veggies (page 67)

Days 2, 3 & 4: Crackers, cheese, tortillas, pouched chicken or tuna,
                small packets of salad dressing (to make chicken or
                tuna salad), dried fruit, and bits of chocolate

DINNERS:

Day 1:	Curried Slaw (page 79)
	Angel Hair Pasta With Shrimp in Cajun-Cream Sauce (page 86)
Day 2:	Mongolian Beef (page 107)
Day 3:	Chicken and Black-Bean Burritos (page 118)
Day 4:	Easy Quesadillas, with pouched chicken added (page 68)

FOUR-DAY VEGETARIAN MENU

BREAKFASTS:

Days 1 & 4:	Kiwi Muesli with Instant Soy Milk (page 45)—V
Day 2:	Jamie's Eggs Durango (page 48)—skip cheese for V
Day 3:	Lemon Poppy Seed Pancakes (page 58)

LUNCHES AND SNACKS:

Day 1:	Hummus With Pita and Veggies (page 67)
Days 2, 3, & 4:	Crackers, cheese, tortillas, trail mix, peanut or other nut butter, dried fruit, and bits of chocolate

DINNERS:

Day 1:	Crunchy Cabbage & Apple Salad (page 76)—V
	Santa Fe Rigatoni (page 88)—V
Day 2:	Kickin' Veggie Stew (page 108)—V
Day 3:	Meaty Vegetarian Chili (page 112) with Cornbread Dumplings (page 73)
Day 4:	Enchilada Pie (page 117)—omit cheese for V

DESSERTS:

Your choice or bring along some dark chocolate.

SEVEN-DAY / SIX-NIGHT TRIP MENU
(CANOE/KAYAK/BASECAMP)

BREAKFASTS:

Days 1, 5, & 7: Kathleen's Cherry-Nut Granola (page 46)

Day 2:   Pumpkin Pancakes (page 59)

Day 3:   Backcountry Pain Perdue with fresh melon (page 54)

Day 4:   Huevos Rancheros (page 47)

Day 6:   Egg Tacos (page 50)

LUNCHES AND SNACKS:

Day 1:   Hummus With Pita and Veggies (page 67)

Day 2 – 6:   Bagels, crackers, cheese, tortillas, peanut butter, apples, summer sausage, pouched chicken and tuna, small packets of salad dressing (for chicken and tuna salad), hard cookies (like ginger snaps or Oreos), dried fruit, and bits of good chocolate

Day 7:   Greek Pasta Salad, prepared the night before (page 81)

DINNERS:

Day 1:   Chicken Fajitas (page 126) with Gonzo Rice (page 74)

Day 2:   Pseudo-Caesar Salad (page 77)

                 Pan-Seared Pork Tenderloin in Cherry Red-Wine Peppercorn Sauce (page 129)

Day 3:   Meaty Vegetarian Chili (page 112) with Cornbread Dumplings (page 73)

                 Use leftover chili in the next morning's Huevos Rancheros

Day 4:   Portabella Mushroom Tortellini With Spicy Sausage (page 94)

Day 5:   Enchilada Pie (page 117)

Day 6:   Greek Cabbage Salad (page 85)

                 Angel Hair Pasta in Smoked Salmon Cream Sauce (page 95)

DESSERTS:

Your choice and bring along some dark chocolate.

Appendix B

Equivalent Measures and Conversion Charts

The charts below use standard U.S. measures. The charts offer equivalents for United States, metric, and Imperial (U.K.) measures. All conversions are approximate and most have been rounded up or down to the nearest whole number.

LIQUID MEASURES

1 jigger (large) = 3 tablespoons = 1½ fluid oz

1 cup = 8 fluid oz = ½ pint = 237 ml

2 cups = 16 fluid oz, 1 pint, 474 ml

4 cups = 32 fluid oz = 1 quart = 946 ml

2 pints = 32 fluid oz = 1 quart = 0.964 liters

4 quarts = 128 fluid oz. = 1 gallon = 3.784 liters

STANDARD MEASURES

1/16 teaspoon = a dash

1/8 teaspoon or less = a pinch or 6 drops = .5 ml

¼ teaspoon = 15 drops = 1 ml

½ teaspoon = 30 drops = 2 ml

1 teaspoon = 1/3 tablespoon = 1/6 oz = 5 ml

1 tablespoon = 3 teaspoons = ½ oz = 14 grams

1/8 cup = 2 tablespoons = 1 oz = 28 grams

¼ cup = 4 tablespoons = 2 oz – 56.7 grams

1/3 cup = 5½ tablespoons = 2.6 oz = 75.6 grams

½ cup = 8 tablespoons = 4 oz = ¼ lb = 113 grams

2/3 cup = 11 tablespoons = 5.2 oz = 151 grams

¾ cup = 12 tablespoons = 6 oz = .375 lb = 170 grams

1 cup = 16 tablespoons = 8 oz = .5 lb = 225 grams

2 cups = 32 tablespoons = 16 oz = 1 lb = 454 grams

4 cups = 1 quart = 64 tablespoons = 2 lbs = 907 grams

BRITISH MEASURES

1 tablespoon English = 4 teaspoons American (1-1/3 American tablespoons)

Dessertspoon (English) = 1 tablespoon American

1 cup English (1/2 pint) = 1¼ cups American

1 pint imperial = 20 fluid oz = 2½ cups American

1 gill = ½ cup American plus 2 American tablespoons

1 gallon imperial = 160 fluid oz = 5 quarts = 20 cups

GRAM-LITER TABLES—DRY-SOLID MEASURES

OUNCES	CONVENIENT EQUIVALENT	GRAMS
.035 oz	1 g	1 g
1 oz	30 g	28.35 g
2 oz	60 g	56.7 g
3 oz	85 g	85.05 g
4 oz	115 g	113.4 g
5 oz	140 g	141.7 g
6 oz	180 g	170.1 g
8 oz	225 g	226.8 g
9 oz	250 g	255.1 g
10 oz	285 g	283.5 g
12 oz	340 g	340.2 g
14 oz	400 g	396.9 g
16 oz	450 g	453.6 g
24 oz	675 g	680.4 g

SUBSTITUTIONS

1 tsp baking powder equals ¼ tsp baking soda + ½ tsp cream of tartar

1 tbsp bouillon equals 1 bouillon cube

1 cup butter equals 7/8 cup vegetable oil

1 tbsp cornstarch equals 2 tbsp all-purpose flour or
4 to 6 teaspoons quick-cooking tapioca

2 tbsp egg, powdered equals 1 egg + 2 tbsp water

1 cup buttermilk equals 1 cup plain yogurt

1 tbsp fresh herbs equals ½ tsp dried herbs

2/3 cup honey equals 1 cup sugar

Equivalent Measures and Conversion Charts

CONVERTING POUNDS TO CUPS

These foods are usually sold by the pound. Here is how to convert to cups when uncooked.

Almonds	1 pound	3 1/3 cups
Apples, dried	1 pound	4 to 5 cups
Apricots, dried	1 pound	3½ to 4 cups
Barley	1 pound	2 ½ cups
Beans, dry (small, such as navy)	1 pound	2 1/3 cups
Beans, dry (large, such as kidney)	1 pound	2½ to 2¾ cups
Beans, black, instant	1 pound	4¾ cups
Beans, refried, instant	1 pound	3½ cups
Biscuit Mix	1 pound	4 cups
Cashews	1 pound	3 1/3 cups
Cheese, cheddar, grated	1 pound	4 to 5 1/3 cups
Cheese, Parmesan, grated	1 pound	5 1/3 cups
Cheese, powdered	1 pound	4 cups
Chili mix	1 pound	3¾ cups
Chocolate chips	1 pound	2 2/3 cups
Cocoa mix	1 pound	6 cups
Coconut	1 pound	5 to 6 cups
Cornmeal	1 pound	3 ¼ cups
Couscous	1 pound	2 2/3 cups
Dates, dried, pitted	1 pound	2½ cups
Eggs, powdered	1 pound	4 cups
Falafel, instant	1 pound	3¼ cups
Flour, unsifted	1 pound	3½ cups
Fruit drink powder, with sugar	1 pound	3 cups
Honey	1 pound	1 1/3 cups
Hummus, instant	1 pound	4 cups
Lentils, dry	1 pound	2 2/3 cups
Macaroni elbows	1 pound	4 cups
Milk, powdered	1 pound	6 cups
Millet	1 pound	2½ cups

Molasses	1 pound	1 1/3 cups
Noodles, egg	1 pound	7 to 9 cups
Nut butters	1 pound	1 2/3 cups
Oatmeal	1 pound	5 cups
Oil	1 pound	2¼ cups
Onion flakes	1 pound	5½ cups
Peaches, dried	1 pound	3 cups
Peanut butter	1 pound	1 2/3 cups
Peas, split, dry	1 pound	2¼ cups
Pecans	1 pound	3½ cups
Potato flakes	1 pound	8 to 10½ cups
Prunes	1 pound	2½ to 3 cups
Raisins	1 pound	2¾ to 3 cups
Rice, brown	1 pound	2 2/3 cups
Rice, instant	1 pound	5 cups
Rice, wild, quick	1 pound	4 cups
Rotini (spirals)	1 pound	6 cups
Sesame seeds	1 pound	3¼ cups
Sour cream powder	1 pound	4 cups
Sugar, granulated	1 pound	2 1/3 cups
Sugar, brown	1 pound	2½ to 3 cups
Sunflower seeds	1 pound	3½ cups
Tahini	1 pound	1 2/3 cups
Tortellini	1 pound	4 cups
Vegetables, dried, mixed	1 pound	6 cups
Walnuts	1 pound	3½ cups
Wheat germ	1 pound	4 cups

Appendix C

SOURCES FOR OUTDOOR GEAR AND COOKWARE

DRIED FRUITS, VEGETABLES, EGGS, MEAT, AND DAIRY
http://store.honeyvillegrain.com/

INSTANT DRY WHOLE MILK
Harder to mix, far superior in taste for travel. Try Nido or Milex brands. These can be sourced on Amazon.com and best rehydrated in a shaker bottle.

ORGANIC FREEZE- AND AIR-DRIED FRUITS AND VEGETABLES
http://www.northbaytrading.com/

http://www.justtomatoes.com/

BAKEPACKER OVEN
www.bakepacker.com
1-866-576-0642

BANKS FRY-BAKE COMPANY
www.frybake.com
1-888-frybake (888-379-2253)

BILLIE COOKWARE
www.jarnaginco.com

GOODWILL
and other secondhand shops are great sources for bakeware on a budget!

GSI OUTDOORS
www.gsioutdoors.com

JETBOIL
www.jetboil.com

L.L. BEAN
www.llbean.com
1-800-441-5713

MOUNTAIN SAFETY RESEARCH (MSR)
www.msrcorp.com

THE OUTBACK OVEN
www.backpackerspantry.com
1-800-641-0500

REI
www.REI.com
1-800-426-4840

SNOW PEAK
www.snowpeak.com

THE WOODY
info@uncommonadv.com
1-866-882-5525

REFERENCES

Cooking the One-Burner Way: Gourmet Cuisine for the Backcountry Chef. Second Edition. Melissa Gray and Buck Tilton. Guilford, CT: The Globe Pequot Press. 2000.

Good Food for Camp and Trail: All-Natural Recipes for Delicious Meals Outdoors. Dorcas S. Miller. Boulder, CO: Pruett Publishing. 1993.

Kayak Cookery: A Handbook of Provisions and Recipes. Linda Daniel. Birmingham, Alabama: Menasha Ridge Press. 1986.

NOLS Cookery (National Outdoor Leadership School). Claudia Pearson, Claudia Lindholm, and Mike Clelland.

NOLS Soft Paths: How to Enjoy the Wilderness Without Harming It. David Cole and Denise Casey. Mechanicsburg, PA: Stackpole Books. 2003.

The One Pan Gourmet: Fresh Food on the trail. Don Jacobson. Camden, ME: Ragged Mountain Press. 1993.

INDEX

176

Uncommon Adventures

Since 1982, Michael Gray has operated Uncommon Adventures, a kayak school and tripping company offering programs in the Great Lakes, Alaska, Central America, and anywhere else you'd care to be inspired. See what new things are simmering at www.uncommonadv.com or phone **1-866-882-5525**.